D0055225

# The Superiority of Christ

# The Superiority of Christ

by
**John MacArthur, Jr.**

MOODY PRESS
CHICAGO

© 1986 by
JOHN F. MACARTHUR, JR.

All rights reserved. No part of this book may be reproduced in any form without permission in writing from the publisher, except in the case of brief quotations embodied in critical articles or reviews.

All Scripture quotations, unless otherwise noted, are from the *New Scofield Reference Bible*, King James Version. Copyright © 1967 by Oxford University Press, Inc. Reprinted by permission.

**Library of Congress Cataloging in Publication Data**

MacArthur, John F.
   The superiority of Christ.

   (John MacArthur's Bible studies)
   Includes index.
      1. Bible. N.T. Hebrews I-II—Criticism, interpre-
tation, etc. 2. Jesus Christ—Person and offices—
Biblical teaching. I. Title. II. Series: MacArthur,
John F. Bible studies.
BS2775.2.M32   1986      227′.8706      86-21727
ISBN 0-8024-5344-9 (pbk.)

1 2 3 4 5 6 Printing/GB/Year 91 90 89 88 87 86

*Printed in the United States of America*

# Contents

These Bible studies are taken from messages delivered by Pastor-Teacher John MacArthur, Jr., at Grace Community Church in Panorama City, California. The recorded messages themselves may be purchased as a series or individually. Please request the current price list by writing to:

WORD OF GRACE COMMUNICATIONS
P.O. Box 4000
Panorama City, CA 91412

Or call the following number:
818-982-7000

# 1

# Introduction to Hebrews

## Outline

Introduction
A. The Particulars of Hebrews
   1. The author
   2. The community
   3. The date
   4. The recipients
      a) Hebrews who were intellectually convinced and committed to Christ
         (1) Their weakness
         (2) Their strength
      b) Hebrews who were intellectually convinced only
         (1) Their ego
         (2) Their exhortation
            (a) Hebrews 2:1-4
            (b) Hebrews 6:4-6
            (c) Hebrews 10:26-27, 29
            (d) Hebrews 12:15-17
      c) Hebrews who were neither convinced nor committed to Christ
   5. The theme
B. The Problems of the Jews
   1. Looking for the perfect priest
      a) Establishing the Old Covenant
      b) Establishing the New Covenant
   2. Letting go of the Old Covenant
      a) An uneasy transition
      b) An intense persecution
   3. Living a better life

Lesson
I. The Preparation for Christ (v. 1)

A. The Accuracy of the Old Testament
   1. The resource
      *a*) Portional revelation
      *b*) Progressive revelation
   2. The recipients
B. The Affirmation of the New Testament
   1. 2 Peter 1:21
   2. 2 Timothy 3:16
II. The Presentation of Christ (v. 2*a*)
   A. Final Revelation
   B. Promised Revelation
   C. Complete Revelation

## Introduction

A good title for the book of Hebrews is "The Superiority of Christ." Jesus Christ is superior to everything and everyone. Hebrews is a tremendous book, but it is difficult to understand. It has many truths that are hard to understand if we are not diligent in our study. Unless you have an intimate knowledge of the Spirit of God and a commitment to understanding the Word of God, you will not understand Hebrews. My former Old Testament professor, Dr. Charles L. Feinberg, said that you cannot understand the book of Hebrews unless you understand the book of Leviticus, because Hebrews is based on the principles of the Levitical priesthood.

A. The Particulars of Hebrews

   1. The author

      Hebrews was written by an unknown author. Some think it was Paul, some Apollos, and some Peter. Personally, I don't believe it was written by Paul. I stand with one of the great teachers of the early church, Origen, who said, "Nobody knows." One thing we do know: it was inspired by the Holy Spirit.

   2. The community

      Hebrews was written to a group of suffering, persecuted Jews outside of Israel. There are no references to Gentiles. The problem of having both Gentile and Jew in the church—a concern in Jerusalem—is not discussed in Hebrews. The letter was written to Jewish believers and unbelievers to reveal the merits of Jesus Christ and the New Covenant as opposed to the Old Covenant.

We do not know the exact location of these Hebrews. They may have been located somewhere near Greece. We do know that this Jewish community had been evangelized by the apostles and prophets soon after Christ's ascension (Heb. 2:3-4).

Included within the framework of the letter are unbelievers within the Jewish community. Unlike Jerusalem or Galilean Jews, they had never met Jesus. Everything they knew about Him they received secondhand. They didn't have the New Testament as it now stands because it had not been put together yet. Whatever they knew they received directly from the apostles and prophets. The recipients of Hebrews were second-generation Christians as a result of apostolic missionaries.

3. The date

The letter to the Hebrews had to have been written sometime after Christ's ascension (about A.D. 30) and sometime before the destruction of Jerusalem (A.D. 70), because the Temple was still standing. I believe the date is somewhere between A.D. 60 and A.D. 69, perhaps about A.D. 65. There had to be time for the apostolic missionaries to evangelize the area. We know that apostolic missionaries were not sent out from Jerusalem for at least seven years after the church had been founded. It was sometime after those seven years before this Jewish community was reached. There also had to have been a certain amount of time for this community to grow spiritually. Hebrews 5:12 says, "When for the time ye ought to be teachers, ye have need that one teach you again the first principles of the oracles of God." The writer was saying that they had had enough time to be mature but were not.

4. The recipients

The critical thing about understanding the book of Hebrews is that there were three basic types of people in view throughout this epistle. For example, if it were written only to Christians, as some have said, then severe problems arise in interpreting passages that could hardly apply to believers. Since it so frequently addresses believers, it could not have been written primarily to unbelievers either. So it must have been written to include both.

*a)* Hebrews who were intellectually convinced and committed to Christ

There was a legitimate congregation of true believers in Jesus Christ in this community. They had been raised in Judaism, but they received Jesus Christ as their Savior. The result was tremendous hostility from their own people. They were ostracized from their families, persecuted by their own countrymen, and suffered greatly.

(1) Their weakness

They should have been mature, but they weren't. They had no confidence. They were in danger of returning to the patterns of Judaism. They were not in danger of losing their salvation, but they were in danger of confusing their salvation with legalism. They couldn't make a clear-cut break between the New Covenant in Christ and all the ceremonies and patterns of their old life in Judaism.

The Hebrew Christians were still hung up on Temple ritual and worship. That's why the Holy Spirit tells them about a new priesthood, a new temple, a new sacrifice, and a new sanctuary that are better than the old ones. These people had gone beyond Judaism by receiving Jesus Christ, but they were still hanging on to many of the Judaistic rituals that had been so much a part of their life. That's understandable, since their friends and countrymen were persecuting them. They were in great danger of creating a ritualistic, legalistic Christianity. They had become a congregation of weaker brothers (Rom. 14:2) who were still calling unclean what the Lord had sanctified (Rom. 14:14).

(2) Their strength

The Holy Spirit directed the book of Hebrews to these weak Christians to strengthen their faith in the New Covenant. They did not need the old Temple, which would be wiped out by Titus Vespasian in a few years, revealing that God was bringing an end to the Old Covenant. They didn't need the old Levitical priesthood. They didn't need the old day-in, day-out sacrifices. They had a new and better covenant with a new and better priesthood, sanctuary, and sacrifice. The book of Hebrews was written to give confidence to those floundering believers.

b) Hebrews who were intellectually convinced only

(1) Their ego

These people knew the truth about Christ but never committed themselves to it. You've probably met people like that—they are intellectually convinced that Christ is who He claimed to be, but they're not willing to put their faith in Him. Why? Because they love the praise of men more than the praise of God (John 12:42-43). They aren't willing to make the sacrifice.

(2) Their exhortation

The Holy Spirit exhorts this group in the book of Hebrews to go all the way to saving faith—to make the necessary commitment.

(a) Hebrews 2:1-4—"We ought to give the more earnest heed to the things which we have heard, lest at any time we should let them slip. For if the word spoken by angels was steadfast, and every transgression and disobedience received a just recompense of reward, how shall we escape, if we neglect so great salvation?" (vv. 1-3). This group of unbelievers was at the point of belief but wouldn't make the commitment. They were guilty of neglecting to do what they had been convinced was right. They should have known better because the truth had been confirmed by the apostles with miracles and gifts of the Holy Spirit (v. 4).

(b) Hebrews 6:4-6—"It is impossible for those who were once enlightened [not saved, but intellectually convinced], and have tasted of the heavenly gift, and were made partakers of the Holy Spirit, and have tasted the good word of God, and the powers of the age to come, if they shall fall away, to renew them again unto repentance, seeing they crucify to

11

themselves the Son of God afresh, and put him to an open shame." When a man is totally convinced that Jesus Christ is who He claimed to be but still refuses to believe in Him, he is without excuse and without hope because he won't put his trust in what he knows to be true. There is nothing else God can do but warn him.

(c) Hebrews 10:26-27, 29—What is the greatest sin a man can commit? Rejecting Christ. Verse 26 says, "If we sin willfully after we have received the knowledge of the truth, there remaineth no more sacrifice for sins." If a man receives the truth, understands it, and is intellectually convinced of it, yet willfully rejects Christ, what can God do? The writer continues, "But a certain fearful looking for of judgment and fiery indignation, which shall devour the adversaries. . . . Of how much sorer punishment, suppose ye, shall he be thought worthy, who hath trodden under foot the Son of God, and hath counted the blood of the covenant, with which he was sanctified, an unholy thing, and hath done despite unto the Spirit of grace?" (vv. 27, 29). When someone knows the truth and rejects it, he will face severe punishment.

(d) Hebrews 12:15-17—"Looking diligently lest any man fail of the grace of God, lest any root of bitterness springing up trouble you, and by it many be defiled; lest there be any fornicator, or profane person, like Esau, who for one morsel of food sold his birthright. For ye know how afterward, when he would have inherited the blessing, he was rejected; for he found no place of repentance, though he sought it carefully with tears." That is the tragedy of making a decision too late—another warning to the individual who has never made a commitment to Christ.

c) Hebrews who were neither convinced nor committed to Christ

This group refers to Israel in general. The Holy Spirit,

in addition to strengthening the faith of Christians and exhorting the intellectually convinced to put their faith in Christ, wanted to show those who were unconvinced that Jesus is in fact who He claimed to be. In Hebrews 9 He speaks through the author of Hebrews to those people: "Christ being come an high priest of good things to come, by a greater and more perfect tabernacle, not made with hands, that is to say, not of this building. . . . How much more shall the blood of Christ, who through the eternal Spirit offered himself without spot to God, purge your conscience from dead works to serve the living God? And for this cause he is the mediator of the new testament, that by means of death, for the redemption of the transgressions that were under the first testament, they who are called might receive the promise of eternal inheritance" (vv. 11, 14-15). Verses 27-28 say, "As it is appointed unto men once to die, but after this the judgment, so Christ was once offered to bear the sins of many; and unto them that look for him shall he appear the second time without sin unto salvation." Those messages were for the unbeliever who needed to know who Christ really is.

Three groups of people are in view in this epistle. The key to interpreting Hebrews is to determine which group the writer is addressing. If we don't understand that, then we will be confused. He is not, for example, telling believers, "It is appointed unto men once to die, but after this the judgment" (Heb. 9:27). The primary flow of the text is to believers, but periodically there are warnings to two groups of unbelievers: the intellectually convinced and the unconvinced. In a masterful way, the Holy Spirit pulls these three groups together to meet every one of their particular needs and answer their questions in the same letter. There is confidence and assurance for the Christian. There are warnings to the intellectually convinced to receive Christ or be damned by his own knowledge. And there is a convincing presentation to the unbelieving, unconvinced Jew that he should believe in Jesus Christ. Hebrews is simply a presentation of Christ as the Messiah—the Author of a New Covenant greater than the one God made in the Old Testament. That is not to say the old one was wrong; it just was incomplete.

5. The theme

The theme of Hebrews is the superiority, or preeminence, of Christ. He is better than any Old Testament person, institution, ritual, or sacrifice.

The book of Hebrews begins with the superiority of Christ to everyone and everything. That's a summary of the entire book, and it's contained in the first three verses. From those verses we move on to the superiority of Christ over angels, over Moses, over Joshua, over Aaron and his priesthood, and over the Old Covenant. From that the book moves to the superiority of Christ's sacrifice over the old sacrifices, of Christ's faithfulness over all the faithless, and of Christ's testimony over the testimony of all others.

B. The Problems of the Jews

1. Looking for the perfect priest

It had always been dangerous for a Jew to approach God. Exodus 33:20 says, "There shall no man see me, and live." Only on the Day of Atonement, which occurred once a year, could the high priest enter the Holy of Holies where dwelt the *Shekinah*—the glory of God's presence. The Jewish people could not see God. They couldn't go near Him except for one day a year, and then only one person could.

a) Establishing the Old Covenant

Since nearness to God was not possible, there had to be a basis for some relationship between God and Israel. So God established a covenant, which means that God, in His grace and sovereign initiative, offered Israel a special relationship with Himself. In a very unique way He would be their God, and they would be His people. They could have special access to Him if they were obedient to His laws. But to break the law was sin, and sin interfered with their access to Him. Since they were always sinning, access was always interrupted. So God instituted a system of sacrifices. The Levitical priesthood offered sacrifices to atone for sin, which removed the barrier so that access to God might be resumed.

How many times did the sacrifices have to be made? Incessantly—hour after hour, day after day, month after month, year after year. Since the priests were

14

sinners also, they too had to make sacrifices for their own sins just to be able to make sacrifices for the sins of the people. So the barrier between God and the people was continually going up and down. The system was imperfect.

b)   Establishing the New Covenant

Mankind needed a perfect priest who could open the way to God once and for all. He needed to perform a perfect sacrifice that didn't just deal with one sin but took away all sin forever. And that, says the writer of Hebrews, is exactly what Jesus did. He became the mediator of a better covenant—better because it didn't have to be repeated every hour (for His sacrifice covered every sin once and for all) and because He's a priest who doesn't need to make any sacrifices for Himself—He's totally perfect. His perfect sacrifice eliminated the penalty of sin for those who would believe.

Hebrews 10:10 says, "By which will we are sanctified [made pure] through the offering of the body of Jesus Christ once for all." That was something new in the sacrificial system. It was a better covenant because one sacrifice accomplished sanctification. Verse 12 says, "But this man, after he had offered one sacrifice for sins forever, sat down." That's something no priest could ever do. They had to keep making sacrifices. Jesus made one, sat down, and it was done. Verse 14 says, "For by one offering, he hath perfected forever them that are sanctified."

Christ is a better priest making a better sacrifice. That is the message of the book of Hebrews to the Jewish people. To the believer the writer says, "Have confidence in the New Covenant." To the intellectually convinced he says, "Receive it; don't fall into perdition when you're only a step away." And to the unbeliever he says, "Look at how much better it is. Receive Christ." All their lives the Jewish people had been looking for the perfect priest and the perfect final sacrifice. The writer tells them that all that is found in Jesus Christ. The superiority of Christ is the theme of the book of Hebrews.

2. Letting go of the Old Covenant

It was extremely difficult for the Jews to accept the superiority of the New Covenant. It was especially hard for them to make a clean break with the Old. The Gentiles didn't have that problem because they had never been a part of the Old. They had lost the knowledge of the true God long before and consequently worshiped idols.

a) An uneasy transition

The Jews always had a divine religion and a divinely appointed place of worship. Difficulty arose for those presenting the truth to the Jew because he would say, "I already know the truth." It was not easy for him to make the transition to Christianity because he saw it as a complete forsaking of his God-authored heritage. It was a natural desire for a Christian Jew to retain some of the forms and ceremonies that were a part of his upbringing. That was part of the problem faced by the writer of Hebrews—confronting the born-again Jew about letting go of his past. That was especially hard for him since the Temple was still standing and the priests were continuing to minister. It became easier after the Temple was destroyed in A.D. 70.

b) An intense persecution

Intense persecution added an extra dimension that made it even more difficult for the Jew to give up the Old Covenant. Ananias, the high priest, banished Christian Jews from the holy places. They could no longer take part in God-appointed services. They were considered unclean. They couldn't go into the Temple and take part in the sacrifices. They couldn't communicate with the priests. And they could have nothing to do with their own people. They were cut off from their society. By clinging to their faith in Jesus as the Messiah, they had been banished from everything they had ever known. They were considered worse than Gentiles, but they were actually the only true Jews. For the true Jew is not one outwardly but inwardly (Rom. 2:28-29).

The Christian Jews were beginning to say to themselves, *This life is rough. We believe in Christ, but it's tough to make the break with the traditions we've held. Is Christ really the Messiah?* Doubt had become a problem. They were spiritually infantile in their thinking, and they didn't have any resources to fall back on.

3. Living a better life

Throughout the book of Hebrews the writer tells the Christians to put their confidence in Christ, who is the mediator of a better covenant and the new, great High Priest. They weren't losing anything; they were gaining something better. They may have been deprived of an earthly Temple, but they were going to get a heavenly one. They had been deprived of an earthly priesthood, but they had a heavenly priest. They had been deprived of the sacrifices, but Christ gave them one final sacrifice. Everything in Hebrews is presented as something better. These phrases are just a sample of those better things: a better hope, a better testament, a better promise, a better sacrifice, a better substance, a better country, and a better resurrection. Hebrews presents Jesus Christ, and we are presented as being in Him—dwelling in a new dimension: the heavenlies. In Hebrews we can read about the heavenly Christ, the heavenly calling, the heavenly gift, the heavenly country, and the heavenly Jerusalem. Everything is new and better. We don't need the old anymore.

A good summary of the book of Hebrews is in chapter 8, verse 1: "Now of the things which we have spoken this is the sum: We have such an high priest, who is seated on the right hand of the throne of the Majesty in the heavens." We have a great High Priest who is seated, and that means His work is done.

The writer of Hebrews wants to show three groups of Jews that Christ is better than anything in the Old Testament and that the New Covenant is better than the Old. Everything they have in Christ is infinitely sufficient. The first three verses of Hebrews show us that Christ is superior to every one and every thing. And that is the theme of the epistle. I want you to see three features: the preparation for Christ, the presentation of Christ, and the preeminence of Christ.


**Lesson**


I. THE PREPARATION FOR CHRIST (v. 1)

"God, who at sundry times and in diverse manners spoke in time past unto the fathers by the prophets."

17

That verse gives us an indication of how God wrote the Old Testament. The purpose of the Old Testament was to prepare God's people for the coming of Christ, whether it be through prophecy, type, principle, or commandment. As marvelous as the senses of man are, they are incapable of reaching beyond the natural world. If we were ever going to know anything about God, it was God who had to speak. Verse 1 says that God "spoke." We could never know God if He did not speak to us.

## The Religion Box

You and I live in a natural box—we are bound by our existence in time and space. Outside our natural box is the supernatural. Deep down, we know the supernatural exists outside of ourselves, but we can't know anything about it on our own. There are people who want to discover the supernatural, so they start a religion. They run to the edge of the box and try to chisel holes in it. They figure that a hole will let them crawl out of the box and find God. The various religions of the world are all trying to accomplish the same thing—to escape the natural and enter the supernatural. But there's one problem: No one can do it. The natural man cannot escape into the supernatural.

You can't go into a phone booth and come out Superman. You cannot transcend your natural existence. If you are ever to know anything about God, it will not be because you escaped to God but because He spoke to you. You cannot discover God. He literally became a man and burst into the box to tell us about Himself. That's what revelation is all about.

Every other religion in the world is man's backward attempt to jump out of the box. But Christianity takes the opposite approach: Jesus said, "The Son of man is come to seek and to save that which was lost" (Luke 19:10). When God burst into the box, He did so in a human form. The name of that human form was Jesus Christ. That's the difference between Christianity and every other religion in the world. Many people think you can believe in any religion you want. However, you won't find God if you do. Every religion is man's attempt to discover God. Christianity is God bursting into man's world and telling man what He is like. Man is incapable of comprehending, identifying, or understanding God at all on his own. God must first invade his world. And He did!

A. The Accuracy of the Old Testament

God first spoke through the words of the Old Testament. Men didn't write it on their own; they were simply instruments. God was the energizing author. Deity is not speechless. The deists have taught that God started the world going and then went away and let it run by itself. But God is not detached or uninvolved. The true and living God, unlike the idols of the heathen, is not a dumb being. The God of Scripture, unlike the impersonal "First Cause" of some philosophers, is not silent. He speaks, and He spoke in the Old Testament. The Old Testament is not the wisdom of man; it is the voice of God.

1. The resource

   *a)* Portional revelation

   Hebrews 1:1 says, "God, who at sundry times [Gk., *polumerōs*] and in diverse manners [Gk., *polutropōs*]." That is a play on words. Those two Greek words respectively mean "in many portions" (different books) and "in many different manners."

   There are thirty-nine books in the Old Testament. That's "many portions"! Sometimes God spoke directly to a man and told him to write. Sometimes He communicated through a vision, sometimes in a parable, and sometimes through a type or a symbol. There are different ways in which God spoke in the Old Testament, but it was always God who spoke. The personalities and minds of the men were used, but they were totally controlled by the Spirit of God. Every word they said was what God decided they should say. Some of the Old Testament is history, some is poetry, some is law, and some is prophecy. God speaks through it all.

   *b)* Progressive revelation

   The Old Testament was fragmentary and incomplete. It was written over a period of fifteen hundred years by more than forty writers, each book having its own element of truth. The Old Testament is progressive revelation. First Genesis gives some truth, then comes Exodus, and it continues to build. It is progressive not in that it goes from error to truth, but in that it goes from incompleteness to a higher state of completeness. It remained incomplete until the New

19

Testament came along. In the Old Testament, God was pleased to dispense His gracious truth to the Jews by the mouths of His prophets in different manners. His revelation started with a lesser degree of light and progressed to a greater degree.

Remember one important thing: Just because the Old Testament was progressive does not mean that it is wrong in any way. There is simply development. For example, the standards of morality established in the Old Testament were totally refined in Jesus. God gave man a progressive revelation. The distinction is not in the nature of the truth; it's in the amount and time of it. Children are first taught letters, then words and sentences. God gave His revelation in the same way. He began with types, ceremonies, and prophecies and progressed to final completion in Christ.

2. The recipients

Hebrews 1:1 says, "God, who at sundry times and in diverse manners spoke in time past unto the fathers by the prophets." God spoke back in the past to the fathers—the Old Testament saints, our spiritual ancestors. He spoke to them by the prophets. They were His messengers. A prophet is one who speaks to men for God; a priest is one who speaks to God for men. The priest took man's problem to God; the prophet took God's message to man.

B. The Affirmation of the New Testament

In verse 1 the Holy Spirit establishes the accuracy of the Old Testament and its divine authorship. And this truth is affirmed throughout the New Testament.

1. 2 Peter 1:21—"The prophecy [the Old Testament] came not at any time by the will of man, but holy men of God spoke as they were moved by the Holy Spirit."

2. 2 Timothy 3:16—"All scripture is given by inspiration of God."

The Old Testament is true. It was the progressive preparation for Jesus Christ.


II. THE PRESENTATION OF CHRIST (v. 2a)

"Hath in these last days spoken unto us by his Son."

A. Final Revelation

This verse describes the finalizing of the revelation. God, who used to speak in many ways and many forms to many people, has finally spoken in one way through one individual—Jesus Christ. The entire New Testament is centered around Christ. The gospels give His story, the epistles comment on it, and the book of Revelation tells about His future. No one prophet was ever able to grasp the whole truth. Only Jesus is the whole truth. The Old Testament was pieces and fragments, but Jesus is full and final revelation.

B. Promised Revelation

Notice in verse 2 the phrase "in these last days." There are several ways to interpret that. The writer could be referring to the last days of revelation, meaning final revelation. There is no question that Christ is the final revelation. He could also be saying that in the last days of revelation, God spoke through His Son. But better than that is the interpretation that the writer is making a Messianic reference. The phrase "the last days" was familiar to the Jew. Since he was writing to Jews, we will take it in that context. Whenever a Jew saw the phrase "the last days," he immediately thought of the Messiah because the promise was given that in the last days, the Messiah would establish His kingdom (Mic. 4:1-2). So the writer is saying Jesus was that Messiah and spoke the final revelation of God. Unfortunately, the Jewish nation as a whole rejected the Messiah. The fulfillment of all the promises of the last days had to be postponed and the age of grace (the church age) intervened instead. In John 4:25 the woman at the well in Sychar says to Jesus, "I know that Messiah cometh, who is called Christ; when he is come, he will tell us all things." She knew that Messiah would unfold the full and final revelation of God—and indeed He did.

C. Complete Revelation

To add anything to the New Testament is blasphemous. Revelation 22:18 says, "If any man shall add unto these things, God shall add unto him the plagues that are written in this book." Verse 19 indicates that if someone takes anything away from it, God will take away his part from the tree of life.

God's final revelation was made in one greater than the prophets—Jesus Christ. The Old Testament was revealed in pieces. To Abraham was revealed the nation of the Messiah; to Jacob, the tribe of the Messiah; to David and Isaiah, the family of the Messiah; to Micah, the town where He would be born; to Daniel, the time when He would be born; and to Malachi, the forerunner who would precede Him. In Jonah His resurrection was typified. Every one of those pieces came together in Jesus Christ. Everything is complete in Him (Col. 2:9-10).

Jesus Christ is greater than the prophets and greater than any revelation in the Old Testament because He is the embodiment of all revelation. God has fully expressed Himself in Christ.

In Hebrews 1:2 the Holy Spirit establishes the superiority of Christ over all the Old Testament prophets—first in character, because the old was fragmentary and the new is perfect; second, the New Covenant is even better because the instruments of revelation in the old were sinful men while the instrument in the new was the Son of God; and third, God's revelation in the past has been completed in the last days. In the first one-and-one- half verses, the Holy Spirit establishes the preeminence of Jesus Christ over all the Old Testament. And that is exactly what the believing and unbelieving Hebrews needed to hear.

Some of you who will read this have never met Jesus Christ as your Savior. Maybe you have put your faith in money, popular- ity, prestige, or success. But Jesus Christ is superior to anything and everything. Peter said, "Neither is there salvation in any other; for there is no other name under heaven given among men, whereby we must be saved" (Acts 4:12). There is no other way to God. Jesus Christ is superior to any method, any religion, or any philosophy. He is the preeminent One. Unless a man puts his faith in Jesus Christ, he is doomed, for it is Christ alone who provides revelation and redemption from God.

### Focusing on the Facts

1. Who wrote the book of Hebrews (see p. 8)?
2. When might Hebrews have been written (see p. 9)?
3. What is critical to a clear understanding of Hebrews (see p. 9)?
4. One group to whom the book of Hebrews was written was Jewish believers. What was the danger they were facing (see p. 10)?
5. Why did the Holy Spirit write Hebrews to that group (see p. 1)?
6. Hebrews was also written to those Jews who were intellectually convinced about Christ. What did the Holy Spirit exhort them to do (see p. 11)?
7. What is the greatest sin a man can commit (Heb. 10:26-27, 29; see p. 12)?

8. What did the Holy Spirit want to show the unconvinced Jews—the third group of people to whom Hebrews was written (see p. 13)?
9. What is the key to interpreting Hebrews (see p. 13)?
10. What is the theme of Hebrews (see p. 14)?
11. How did God establish a relationship with the nation of Israel when physical nearness to Him was not possible for the people (see p. 14)?
12. Why was the covenant that Christ mediated better than the old one (see p. 15)?
13. Why was it difficult for many of the Jewish people to accept the New Covenant as superior to the Old (see p. 16)?
14. What are some of the better things that the New Covenant in Christ offered the Jew (see p. 17)?
15. What is a good summary of the book of Hebrews (Heb. 8:1; see p. 17)?
16. Since man is incapable of reaching beyond the natural world to God, how is man able to reach God (see p. 18)?
17. What is the difference between the religions of man and Christianity (see p. 18)?
18. How did God first speak to man (see p. 19)?
19. What are some of the different ways in which God communicated to the writers of the Old Testament (see p. 19)?
20. Why is the Old Testament considered to be progressive revelation (see pp. 19-20)?
21. Describe the difference between a prophet and a priest (see p. 20).
22. What does the phrase "in these last days" refer to in Hebrews 1:2 (see p. 21)?

## Pondering the Principles

1. Since some understanding of the book of Leviticus would be helpful to understanding the book of Hebrews, plan to read Leviticus over the next week. There are twenty-seven chapters, so you could easily read four chapters each day. If there is an outline of Leviticus in your Bible, follow along with it so you understand the flow of thought. If not, make your own outline as you read.

2. The people of Israel had to offer many continual sacrifices to atone for their sin and restore their relationship with God. But Christ made one final sacrifice that took away all sin and opened the way to God for all of us. Spend time in prayer right now by thanking Christ for His sacrifice on your behalf. Thank Him for

the salvation He has given you and the access you now have to God.

3. Throughout Hebrews the writer discusses differences between the New and the Old Covenant. He tells us how much better the New is. Make a plan to read through Hebrews, and as you read, make a list of those things. When you have finished your list, review it. Then thank God for His establishment of the New Covenant in Christ.

# 2
# The Preeminence of Christ

**Outline**

Introduction

Review
I. The Preparation of Christ (v. 1)
II. The Presentation of Christ (v. 2a)

Lesson
III. The Preeminence of Christ (vv. 2b-3)
  A. His Heirship (v. 2b)
    1. The passages
      a) Psalm 2:6-9
      b) Psalm 89:27
      c) Romans 11:36
    2. The proof
    3. The price
    4. The partnership
    5. The parable
  B. His Act of Creation (v. 2c)
    1. An infinite creation
    2. An improbable evolution
  C. His Brightness (v. 3a)
    1. The manifestation of God
    2. The light of the world
  D. His Being (v. 3b)
    1. Colossians 1:15
    2. Colossians 1:19
    3. Colossians 2:9
  E. His Administration (v. 3c)
    1. Upholding the earth
      a) Avoiding chaos
      b) Maintaining the cosmos
    2. Upholding His people

F. His Sacrifice (v. 3*d*)
   1. The ransom
      *a*)  Hebrews 7:27
      *b*)  Hebrews 9:12-14, 26
      *c*)  1 Peter 1:18-19
      *d*)  1 John 1:7
   2. The rejection
G. His Exaltation (v. 3*e*)
   1. The stature
   2. The signs
      *a*)  Honor
      *b*)  Rule
      *c*)  Rest
      *d*)  Intercession

## Introduction

In the first three verses of Hebrews the writer introduces the person of Jesus Christ. The theme for the epistle is the superiority and preeminence of Christ. There is no other like Him—everything and everyone else comes under Him.

## Review

Hebrews is a marvelous letter from an unknown writer sent primarily to a congregation of Jewish believers living somewhere outside the land of Israel. They had evidently been won to Christ by apostolic missionaries. The bulk of the epistle is directed toward Christians, but throughout it there are at least five parenthetical warnings to unbelievers—to either those who knew the truth and were rejecting it or those who hadn't yet understood the truth. So whether the writer was directing the epistle to an unbeliever or a believer, he was constantly announcing the superiority of Christ. Even the Jewish Christians were in danger of remaining attached to the Old Covenant. He wanted them to understand that they didn't need it anymore because Christ is all sufficient. Thus Hebrews became a reminder to the Jewish Christians of the glories of the Savior. It was an encouragement for them to know that the New Covenant is better than the Old. The Jewish believer did not have to hold onto the Old Covenant; he could let go and grow to maturity in Christ in the New Covenant.

Scattered throughout Hebrews are at least five parenthetical warnings to Jewish unbelievers of the consequences of rejecting the preeminence of Christ and the New Covenant. Fitting into the theme of the exaltation of Jesus Christ, the opening verses are high and lofty. They establish at the beginning of the epistle His absolute and total preeminence. Jesus Christ is superior to everything and everyone in existence.

I. THE PREPARATION OF CHRIST (v. 1; see pp. 17-20)

II. THE PRESENTATION OF CHRIST (v. 2a; see pp. 20-22)

In the Old Testament, God spoke in many ways and many forms through many different individuals. In the New Testament, God speaks through His Son. The writers of the New Testament are either historians or commentators on God's Son—either recording the history of the life of Christ or the principles laid down by Christ. He is the New Testament, which is the revelation of Christ.

## Fulfilling the Old Testament

The transition of revelation from the Old Testament to the New Testament is called progressive revelation. The Old Testament was promise; the New Testament is fulfillment. Christ said, "I am not come to destroy [the Law], but to fulfill" (Matt. 5:17). The Old Testament clearly indicates that the men of faith who were writing it were trusting in a promise that was yet to come.

1.  Hebrews 11:39-40—This chapter of Hebrews describes the heroes of faith of the Old Testament. The writer says, "And these all, having received witness through faith, received not the promise, God having provided some better thing for us, that they without us should not be made perfect." The Old Testament saints never saw the fulfillment of the promise. They wrote down what was going to happen without seeing it fully realized.

2.  1 Peter 1:10-12—The apostle Peter said the authors of the Old Testament tried hard to understand their own writings: "Of which salvation the prophets have inquired and searched diligently, who prophesied of the grace that should come unto you, searching what [person], or what manner of time the Spirit of Christ who was in them did signify, when he testified beforehand the sufferings of Christ, and the glory that should follow. Unto whom it was revealed that, not unto themselves but unto us they did minister the things which are

27

now reported unto you by them that have preached the gospel." In the Old Testament the prophets wrote about the unfulfilled promise and then read what they wrote to try to figure out what it meant. They knew nothing of the fulfillment of what they wrote.

Progressive revelation began in the Old Testament with a promise and ended in the New Testament with the fulfillment of God's Son.

No religion can give us the Word of God. Peter said that there is no salvation in any other than Jesus Christ (Acts 4:12). Hebrews 1:2 says, "[God] hath in these last days spoken unto us by his Son." God has spoken finally and exclusively in Jesus Christ. What will happen to people who believe in a religion? If they do not hear what God says in the person of Jesus Christ then they do not hear God at all.

According to Jeremiah 23:21-22 and Amos 3:7, true prophets were let in on the secrets of God. They often wrote those secrets down without understanding them, but in Jesus Christ they are all understood. He is the fulfillment—He is God's final word. Second Corinthians 1:20 says, "All the promises of God in him are yea, and in him Amen, unto the glory of God by us." Every promise resolves itself in Christ, thus He is the final revelation.

Notice that Hebrews 1:2 says, "Hath in these last days." What are the "last days"? Those are the days of the fulfillment of all promises. The Jewish nation saw the last days as the time when the Messiah, the kingdom, and salvation would come and Israel would no longer be under bondage. Jesus came to fulfill the promises. And although the promise of the kingdom has been postponed, the age of fulfillment began when Jesus arrived. It won't be completed until we enter into the eternal heavens with Christ. The Old Testament age of promise ended when Jesus arrived.

Jesus Christ is no mere man—He is the climax of revelation from God. God fully expressed Himself in Christ.


**Lesson**


III. THE PREEMINENCE OF CHRIST (vv. 2b-3)

In this brief but potent section the Holy Spirit exalts Christ as the full and final revealed expression of God—as more exalted, more

28

excellent, and far superior to anyone or anything. In these verses He tells us that Christ is the end of all things, the beginning of all things, and the middle of all things.

Who is Jesus Christ? There are some people who think He was a good teacher. Other people think He was a religious fanatic. Some others say He was a fake. Others think He was a criminal, a phantom, or a political revolutionary. Some people say He was the highest form of human life—that He had a spark of divinity within Him. There are many explanations about who Jesus was, but I want you to hear what God says about who He is. God gives His answer in a seven-fold presentation of the excellencies of Christ.

A. His Heirship (v. 2*b*)

"Whom he hath appointed heir of all things."

The first thing we learn about Jesus Christ is that He is the heir of all things. Colossians 1:16 says that all things were created by Him and for Him. If Jesus is the Son of God then He is the heir of all that God possesses.

1.  The passages

    *a*)  Psalm 2:6-9—"Yet have I set my king upon my holy hill of Zion. I will declare the decree: The Lord hath said unto me, Thou art my Son; this day have I begotten thee. Ask of me, and I shall give thee the nations for thine inheritance, and the uttermost parts of the earth for thy possession. Thou shalt break them with a rod of iron; thou shalt dash them in pieces like a potter's vessel." The psalmist indicated that God would have a Son who would become the heir of all that He possessed. That Son is Jesus Christ.

    *b*)  Psalm 89:27—"I will make him my firstborn, higher than the kings of the earth." The word *firstborn* does not mean that Jesus Christ didn't exist at one time. The issue is that the firstborn has the right to the inheritance. In this case it's not a chronological term; it's a term of legal right. Christ is God's heir.

    *c*)  Romans 11:36—"For of him, and through him, and to him, are all things: to whom be glory forever. Amen."

Everything that exists, exists for Jesus Christ. He is the heir of all things. That He is lifted to that plane is a testimony of His equality with God. It is beyond human

29

understanding to imagine that the Galilean carpenter who was crucified like a common criminal, naked and bleeding on a cross outside the city of Jerusalem, is the King of kings and Lord of lords.

2.  The proof

    In Revelation 5, God is pictured sitting on a throne holding the scroll that is the title deed to the earth. He is keeping it for His heir. In verse 1 the apostle John says, "And I saw in the right hand of him that sat on the throne a scroll written within and on the back, sealed with seven seals." It was law in Roman times that a will had to be sealed seven times. The apostle John then says, "And I saw a strong angel proclaiming with a loud voice, Who is worthy to open the scroll, and to loose its seals? And no man in heaven, nor in earth, neither under the earth, was able to open the scroll, neither to look on it. And I wept much, because no man was found worthy to open and to read the scroll, neither to look on it. And one of the elders saith unto me, Weep not; behold, the Lion of the tribe of Judah, the Root of David, hath prevailed to open the scroll, and to loose its seven seals. And I beheld and, lo, in the midst of the throne and of the four living creatures, and in the midst of the elders, stood a Lamb as though it had been slain, having seven horns and seven eyes, which are the seven spirits of God sent forth into all the earth. And he came and took the scroll out of the right hand of him that sat upon the throne" (vv. 2-7). Why? Because He had a right to take it. He is the heir of the earth. John's vision in Revelation 5 prophecies that Jesus Christ will someday come and take the scroll out of the Father's hand to inherit the earth.

    In Revelation 6 the tribulation begins as Christ takes back the earth that is rightfully His. One by one He unrolls the seals. As each seal is broken, He takes further possession of His inheritance. Finally, "The seventh angel sounded; and there were great voices in heaven, saying, The kingdom of this world is become the kingdom of our Lord, and of his Christ, and he shall reign forever and ever" (Rev. 11:15). When the seventh trumpet sounds after the seventh seal has been unrolled, the earth will belong to Christ.

3.  The price

    Jesus Christ is the rightful heir to all God has. Hebrews

30

1:2 says, "[God] hath appointed [Christ] heir of all things." The Bible says that when He came to earth, He became poor for our sakes that we through His poverty might be made rich (2 Cor. 8:9). When Christ came to earth, He had nothing for Himself—He didn't even have a place to lay His head (Luke 9:58). His clothes were taken from Him, and He was buried in a grave that didn't belong to Him. On earth He was poor for our sakes, but one day He will inherit all things. According to Philippians 2:11, all will acknowledge Jesus as King.

In Acts 2:36 Peter says, "Let all the house of Israel know assuredly, that God hath made that same Jesus, whom ye have crucified, both Lord and Christ." The carpenter from Galilee who died on a cross is the King of kings and Lord of lords. He will rule the world. Even Satan knows that. When Satan tempted Christ in the wilderness, he tried to get Christ to bow down to him and claim the world by the wrong method. But Jesus didn't have to do that. He is the heir of God's inheritance, which was secured by God's promise.

4. The partnership

According to Romans 8:16-17, you and I will be joint heirs with Christ. When we enter into His eternal kingdom, we will jointly possess all He possesses.

5. The parable

Although Jesus is the heir of all that God possesses, amazingly some still reject Him. Many rejected God as He was revealed in the Old Testament. Now God speaks in the New Testament through His Son, and they continue to reject Him.

Matthew 21:33-44 is a tragic parable. Jesus says, "There was a certain householder, who planted a vineyard, and hedged it round about, and dug a winepress in it, and built a tower, and leased it to tenant farmers, and went into a far country. And when the time of the fruit drew near, he sent his servants to the farmers, that they might receive the fruits of it. And the farmers took his servants, and beat one, and killed another, and stoned another. Again, he sent other servants more than the first; and they did the same unto them. But last of all he sent unto them his son, saying, They will reverence my son. But when the farmers saw the son, they said among themselves, This is the heir; come, let us kill him, and let us seize on his inheritance. And they caught him, and cast him out of the vineyard, and slew him. When the lord, therefore, of the vineyard cometh, what will he do unto those farmers? They say unto him, He will miserably destroy those wicked men, and will lease his vineyard unto other farmers, who shall render him the fruits in their seasons. Jesus saith unto them, Did ye never read in the scriptures, The stone which the builders rejected, the same is become the head of the corner; this is the Lord's doing, and it is marvelous in our eyes? Therefore say I unto you, The kingdom of God shall be taken from you, and given to a nation bringing forth the fruits of it. And whosoever shall fall on this stone shall be broken, but on whomsoever it shall fall, it will grind him to powder."

To willfully reject Jesus Christ, as the world did when it crucified Him, brings about damnation and destruction from a vengeful God. Since Israel not only killed the prophets, but also the Son, the promise was taken from them and given to a new nation, the church. Israel was set aside until the time of its restoration. How tragic it is that although Jesus Christ is clearly the final revelation of God—the ultimate King of kings and Lord of lords—men constantly reject Him, crucifying Him again, and putting Him to an open shame (Heb. 6:6).

B. His Act of Creation (v. 2c)

"By whom also he made the worlds."

Christ is the agent through whom God created the world. John 1:3 says, "All things were made by him; and without him was not anything made that was made." Jesus Christ is the agent of creation.

1. An infinite creation

Jesus had the ability to create, and that set Him apart from men. Only God can create; we can't. If you could create, you'd live in a different house, drive a different car, and probably have a different job—if you had any job at all. You could just sit in your backyard and make money. It's a good thing that God didn't give depraved men the right to create. The ability to create belongs to God, and that Jesus creates indicates He is God and establishes His absolute superiority over everything. He created everything material and everything spiritual.

32

Man has stained His good creation with sin. Even creation groans to be restored to what it was in the beginning (Rom. 8:22).

The end of verse 2 says, "By whom also he made the worlds." The common Greek word for world is *kosmos*, but that is not the word used here. *Aiōnas*, which means "the ages," is used in verse 2. Jesus Christ is responsible for creating not only the physical earth but also time, space, force, action, and matter. The writer of Hebrews does not restrict Christ's creation to this earth; he shows us that Christ is the Creator of the entire universe and of existence itself. And Christ made it all without effort.

2. An improbable evolution

Sir John Eccles, nobel laureate in neurophysiology, said that the odds against the right combination of circumstances occurring to have evolved intelligent life on earth are highly improbable; nevertheless, he went on to say that he believed that such did occur but could never happen again on any planet or in any solar system! ("Evolution and the Conscious Self," *The Human Mind*, ed. John D. Roslansky [Amsterdam: North-Holland, 1967]). His strange logic demonstrates the dilemma of humanistic science. If you don't recognize God as the Creator, then you have problems trying to explain how this universe came into being.

Man thinks he came out of some primeval slime—even though no one knows where the slime came from. A man's heart beats 800 million times in a normal lifetime and pumps enough blood to fill a string of tank cars on a railroad track from New York to Boston. A tiny cubic half inch of brain cells contains all the memories of a lifetime. The ear transfers air waves through fluid and transmits sound. Can a creature that does that be some kind of a cosmic accident?

**Millions, Billions, Trillions**

A. K. Morrison, another scientist, tells us that conditions for life on earth demand so many billions of minute interrelated circumstances appearing simultaneously, in the same infinitesimal moment, that such a prospect becomes beyond belief and beyond possibility.

Consider the vastness of our universe. If you could bore a hole in the sun and somehow put in 1.2 million earths, you would still have room for 4.3 million moons. The sun is 865,000 miles in diameter and 93 million miles away from earth. Our next nearest star is Alpha Centauri, and it is five times larger than our sun. The moon is only 211,453 miles away, and you could walk to it in twenty-seven years. A ray of light travels at 186,000 miles per second, so a beam of light would reach the moon in only one-and-a-half seconds. If we could travel at that speed, we would reach Venus in two minutes and eighteen seconds because it's only 26 million miles away. After four-and-one-half minutes we would have passed Mercury, which is 50 million miles away. We could travel to Mars in four minutes and twenty-one seconds because it's only 34 million miles away. The next stop would be Jupiter— 367 million miles away—and it would take us thirty-five minutes. Saturn is twice as far as Jupiter—790 million miles—and it would take one hour and eleven seconds. Eventually we would pass Uranus, Neptune, and finally Pluto—2.7 billion miles away. Having gotten that far, we still haven't left our solar system, which moves in a multimillion-mile orbit through endless space. The nearest star is ten times further than the boundaries of our solar system—20 billion miles away. The North Star is 400 hundred billion miles away, but that still isn't very far compared with known space. The star called Betelgeuse is 880 quadrillion miles from us and has a diameter of 250 million miles, which is greater than the earth's orbit.

Where did it all come from? Who made it? It can't be an accident. Someone made it, and the Bible tells us it was Jesus Christ. He is the creator who not only created the universe but also can create new life in a man's soul. Second Corinthians 5:17 says, "If any man be in Christ, he is a new creation."

C.  His Brightness (v. 3a)

   "Who [Christ], being the brightness of his [God's] glory."

   1.  The manifestation of God

       The Greek word for "brightness" is *apaugasma*, which means "to send forth light." Jesus is the manifestation of God—He expresses God to us. No one can see God at any time (John 1:18), and none of us ever will. Just as the rays of the sun give light, warmth, life, and growth to the earth, so Jesus Christ is the glorious light of God shining into the hearts of men. The brightness of the sun is the same nature as the sun—it's as old as the sun, and the sun has never been without its brightness. The brightness cannot be separated from the sun. The same is true of Christ in relation to God. He is of the same nature as God, He is as old as God, He has never been without God or God without Him, and He can never be separated from God. Yet the brightness of the sun is not the sun, and neither is Jesus God in that sense. He is fully and absolutely God, yet is a distinct person. Jesus Christ is the brightness of God's essence manifested to men.

2.  The light of the world

    We would never know what God was like if we didn't have Jesus to look at. In John 8:12 Jesus says, "I am the light of the world; he that followeth me shall not walk in darkness, but shall have the light of life." Jesus Christ is the brightness of God's glory, and He can transmit that light into our lives so that we can radiate the glory of God. We live in a dark world. The darkness of injustice, failure, privation, separation, disease, and death surrounds us. A moral darkness exists as men are blinded by their godless appetites and passions. God sent His ray of light, Jesus Christ, into this dark world.

    In 2 Corinthians 4:6 the apostle Paul says that "God, who commanded the light to shine out of darkness, hath shone in our hearts, to give the light of the knowledge of the glory of God in the face of Jesus Christ." When God comes into your life, He gives you light so you can understand His glory. In verse 4, Paul says this about the problem of man: "The god of this age hath blinded the minds of them who believe not, lest the light of the glorious gospel of Christ, who is the image of God, should shine unto them." God sent His rays to man's world in the person of Jesus Christ that man might behold His light and His glory, and that he might know and radiate that light. But Satan has blinded the minds of men to prevent the light of the glorious gospel from shining on them. What a tremendous thing it is to realize that Jesus Christ, who is the full expression of God in human history, can come into my life and give me light in the darkness of this world—light to know and under- stand God, to know life and purpose and meaning, and to know happiness, peace, joy, and fellowship for all eternity.

D. His Being (v. 3*b*)

"The express image of his [God's] person."

Jesus Christ is the express image of God's person. Christ was not only God manifest but also God in substance. The Greek word for the term "express image" is used in classical Greek to indicate a die or a stamp, or the mark made by a seal. In verse 3 it means that Jesus Christ is the exact reproduction of God. When a die is stamped, it gives an exact imprint. Jesus Christ is the reproduction of God in human form.

Notice also that verse 3 says, "The express image of his person." The Greek word for "person" means "substance" or "essence." Christ is the perfect essence of God—the personal imprint of God in time and space.

1. Colossians 1:15—"[Christ] is the image of the invisible God." The Greek word for "image" is *eikōn*, which means "a precise copy," "a reproduction," or "an exact image." To call Christ the *eikōn* of God means He is the exact reproduction of God.

2. Colossians 1:19—"It pleased the Father than in him [Christ] should all fullness dwell."

3. Colossians 2:9—"In him [Christ] dwelleth all the fullness of the Godhead bodily."

Christ was not only God manifest but also God in essence. Christ is God, yet He is distinct in His own person. In spite of that, men continue to reject Him. They continue to remain blind, never knowing God, and being forever separated from God and all that is good and gracious.

E. His Administration (v. 3*c*)

"Upholding all things by the word of his power."

Jesus Christ made all things and will someday inherit all things. He holds them together in the meantime.

1. Upholding the earth

The word *upholding* means "supporting" or "maintaining." It's used in the present tense, implying continuous action. Everything in the universe is sustained at this moment by Jesus Christ.

*a)* Avoiding chaos

Our lives depend on the constancy of physical laws. When an earthquake occurs and shifts things a bit, that's cause for concern or panic, depending on the severity of the quake. Can you imagine what would happen if Jesus Christ relinquished His sustaining power to the laws of the earth and the universe? We would go out of existence. Even if He simply stopped maintaining the law of gravity, we would all die. If the laws of science varied, we couldn't exist. The food you eat could turn to poison. You wouldn't be able to stay on the earth—you'd fall off, if you weren't drowned by the ocean first.

Consider what would happen if things changed. The sun has a surface temperature of twelve thousand degrees fahrenheit. If it were any closer to earth, we'd burn; and if it were any further, we'd freeze. Our globe is tilted on an exact angle of 23 degrees, which enables us to have four seasons. If it weren't tilted, vapors from the ocean would move north and south, eventually piling up monstrous continents of ice. If the moon did not remain a specific distance from the earth, the ocean tide would completely inundate the land twice a day. If the ocean floor merely slipped a few feet deeper, the carbon dioxide and oxygen balance in the earth's atmosphere would be completely upset, and no vegetable or animal life could exist on earth. If our atmosphere suddenly thinned out, the meteors that now harmlessly burn up when they hit our atmosphere would constantly bombard us.

*b)* Maintaining the cosmos

Things don't happen in our universe by accident. Jesus Christ sustains the universe. He is the principle of cohesion. He is not the deist's watchmaker creator who made the world, set it in motion, and hasn't bothered with it since. The reason the universe is a cosmos and not chaos—an ordered and reliable system instead of an erratic and unpredictable muddle— is the upholding power of Jesus Christ.

Scientists who think they are discovering great truths are doing nothing more than discovering the sustaining laws that Christ uses to control the world. No scientist—no mathematician, astronomer, or nuclear physicist—could do anything without the upholding power of Jesus Christ.

Jesus Christ monitors and sustains the movements and developments of the universe, for the entire universe hangs on the arm of Jesus. His unsearchable wisdom and boundless power are manifested in the governing of the universe. And He upholds it all by the word of His power.

2. Upholding His people

When I think about Christ's power to uphold the universe, I realize that it affects my personal life. Philippians 1:6 says, "He who hath begun a good work in you will perform it until the day of Jesus Christ." When Christ begins a work in your heart, He doesn't end there. Jude 24-25 says, "Unto him that is able to keep you from falling, and to present you faultless before the presence of his glory with exceeding joy, to the only wise God, our Savior be glory and majesty, dominion and power, both now and forever." When you give your life to Jesus Christ, He can take you to the end of your life and make sure that you are in God's presence because He constantly sustains your life. He upholds you. A life that is not sustained by Christ is chaos.

F. His Sacrifice (v. 3d)

"When he had by himself purged our sins."

1. The ransom

The Bible says, "The wages of sin is death" (Rom. 6:23). Jesus Christ went to the cross, died the death we deserved, and consequently freed us from the penalty of sin. The creation of the world and the upholding of it are wondrous works, but an even greater work is the purging of the sins of men.

a) Hebrews 7:27—"Who needeth not daily, as those high priests, to offer up sacrifice, first for his own sins and then for the people's; for this he did once, when he offered up himself." In the Old Testament, the priests had to make continual sacrifices, but Jesus made only one. He was not only the priest, but also the sacrifice in that He purged our sins—something the Old Testament sacrifices could not do.

b) Hebrews 9:12-14, 26—"Neither by the blood of goats and calves, but by his own blood he entered in once into the holy place, having obtained eternal redemption for us. For if the blood of bulls and of goats, and the ashes of an heifer sprinkling the unclean, sanctifieth to the purifying of the flesh, how much more shall the blood of Christ, who through the eternal Spirit offered himself without spot to God, purge your conscience from dead works to serve the living God? . . . But now once, in the end of the ages, hath he appeared to put away sin by the sacrifice of himself."

God couldn't communicate with us and we couldn't enter into fellowship with Him unless sin was dealt with, so Christ went to the cross, bore the penalty of sin for all who accept His sacrifice, believe in Him, and receive Him. That's a tremendous statement for the writer of Hebrews to make when you consider the identity of his readers. He was writing to Jewish people to whom the cross was a stumbling block. But he doesn't apologize for the cross; he makes it one of the seven excellent glories of Christ.

c)  1 Peter 1:18-19—"Ye know that ye were not redeemed with corruptible things, like silver and gold, from your vain manner of life received by tradition from your fathers, but with the precious blood of Christ, as of a lamb without blemish and without spot."

d)  1 John 1:7—"We have fellowship one with another, and the blood of Jesus Christ, his Son, cleanseth us from all sin." Jesus came as the perfect sacrifice. You and I are sinners. Either we pay for our own sin, or we allow Jesus Christ to pay for it. God decided to send His Son to die and to cleanse sin. If it is your desire to receive Jesus Christ as Savior, to believe and to accept His sacrifice, then your sins are washed away. The Bible says that without the shedding of blood, there is no remission of sin (Heb. 9:22). The blood of Jesus Christ will never be applied to you unless you receive Christ into your life by faith.

2.  The rejection

The basis of salvation is the shed blood of Christ, which purges sin. Yet there are still people who reject that. Hebrews 10:26 is a warning to them: "For if we sin willfully after we have received the knowledge of the truth, there remaineth no more sacrifice for sins." If you reject Jesus Christ, there is nothing in the universe that

39

can take away your sin, and you will die in your sin (John 8:24).

G. His Exaltation (v. 3e)

"[Christ] sat down on the right hand of the Majesty on high [God]."

The right hand of God is His side of power, and Jesus took His place there.

1. The stature

The significant thing about the last statement of verse 3 is that Jesus sat down. That was contrary to everything the priesthood stood for in the Old Testament. There were no seats in the sanctuary. The priest's work was never finished so he never had time to sit down—he was always making sacrifice day in and day out. But Jesus offered one sacrifice, finished it, and then went to the Father and sat down. What couldn't be accomplished in all the Old Testament sacrifices was accomplished once by Jesus Christ for all time.

2. The signs

What does it mean that He sat down? It means He was exalted and is a sign of many things.

a) Honor

Jesus was seated at the right hand of the Father, and that is the honored seat.

b) Rule

First Peter 3:22 says that Christ "is gone into heaven, and is on the right hand of God, angels and authorities and powers being made subject unto him."

c) Rest

Hebrews 10:12 says, "But this man, after he had offered one sacrifice for sins forever, sat down on the right hand of God."

d) Intercession

According to Romans 8:34, Christ is seated at the right hand of the Father making intercession for us.

We have seen God's portrait of Jesus Christ. He is preeminent in all His roles. We've seen Him as a prophet—the final spokesman for God. We've seen Him as a priest atoning and interceding for us. We've seen Him as King controlling, sustaining, and being seated on a throne. Anyone who says Jesus Christ is anything less than that is a fool. God says that He is preeminent in all things. What does that mean to you? To receive Jesus Christ is to enter into all that He is and has, but to reject Him is to be shut out from His presence into an eternal hell. There are no other choices.

## Focusing on the Facts

1. Define progressive revelation (see p. 27).
2. Did the men of faith understand their writings? Support your answer with Scripture (see pp. 27-28).
3. Who is the heir of all that God possesses (Heb. 1:2; see p. 29)?
4. Explain the meaning of "firstborn" as it is used in Psalm 89:27 (see p. 29).
5. When does Christ take the earth as His inheritance (Rev. 11:15; see p. 30)?
6. What did Christ do to make us rich? Explain (2 Cor. 8:9; see p. 31).
7. What will happen to those who continue to reject Jesus Christ (Matt. 21:44; see pp. 31-32)?
8. What does it mean that Christ "made the worlds" (Heb. 1:2; see p. 33)?
9. Explain how Christ is to God as the brightness is to the sun (see pp. 34-35).
10. Why do men have a problem in trying to see God's light (2 Cor. 4:4; see p. 35)?
11. What did the writer of Hebrews mean when he said that Christ is the "express image" of God's person (Heb. 1:3; see p. 36)?
12. What are some of the things that could happen were Christ to relinquish His sustaining power of the universe (see pp. 36-37)?
13. What effect does Christ's sustaining power have on your personal life (see p. 38)?
14. Name a greater work of Christ than His creation of the world or His sustaining of it (Heb. 1:3; see p. 38).
15. What must a person do before the blood of Christ can ever be applied to his life (see p. 39)?
16. What is significant about the fact that Christ sat down (Heb. 1:3; see p. 40)?
17. Hebrews 1:3 says that Christ "sat down on the right hand of the Majesty." What does that signify (see p. 40)?

## Pondering the Principles

1. Read Hebrews 11:39-40 and 1 Peter 1:10-12. What couldn't the prophets see that you can? How should that advantage help you

to live your Christian life? How should that advantage affect your study of God's Word? Make sure you take advantage of what you know.

2. According to 2 Corinthians 8:9, we were made rich through Christ's poverty. In what ways has Christ made you rich? According to Romans 8:16-17, we have become joint heirs with Christ. Thank God for all you have been given for which you did not have to work. Thank Christ for paying the penalty that you deserved and allowing you to be a joint heir with Him.

3. In John 8:12 Jesus says, "I am the light of the world; he that followeth me shall not walk in darkness, but shall have the light of life." We have the great opportunity of transmitting Christ's light to the world. On a scale of 1-10, rate your success at reflecting His light to the unsaved world. Can unbelievers determine that you are a Christian by your behavior? Pray about your Christian walk. Ask God to help you to reflect His glory. Remember, Satan has blinded unbelievers to prevent them from seeing God's glory, so counteract that by being sure to reflect His glory.

# 3
# Jesus Christ, Superior to Angels— Part 1

**Outline**

Introduction
A.  The Biblical View of Angels
   1.  Their appearance
   2.  Their creation
   3.  Their attributes
     *a*)  Intelligence
     *b*)  Emotion
     *c*)  Speech
     *d*)  Swiftness
   4.  Their home
   5.  Their number
   6.  Their power
   7.  Their organization
   8.  Their ministry
B.  The Jewish View of Angels
   1.  Mediated between God and man
   2.  Acted as God's senate
   3.  Were assigned special tasks
   4.  Gave the Old Testament to Israel
     *a*)  The proof
       (1)  Acts 7:51-53
       (2)  Galatians 3:19
     *b*)  The perversion

Lesson
I.  His Title (vv. 4-5)
A.  The Establishment of Sonship
B.  The Prophecies of Sonship
C.  The Time of Sonship
   1.  It is excellent
   2.  It is not eternal

D. The Fullness of Sonship
 1. His virgin birth
  a) Luke 1:35
  b) Luke 3:22
 2. His resurrection
  a) Romans 1:3-4
  b) Acts 13:33
II. His Worship (v. 6)
 A. His Position
  1. Defined
  2. Dignified
 B. His Return
  1. The destination of Christ
  2. The day of return
  3. The desire of the angels
  4. The delight of worship

## Introduction

The book of Hebrews is written primarily to Jewish believers but also to Jewish unbelievers. The writer wants to convince both groups that the New Covenant is better than the Old—that Jesus Christ is the better priest and better mediator and that He is the final priest and final sacrifice. Throughout Hebrews the writer presents comparisons between the New and Old Covenants and between Jesus Christ and everyone else to show that He is superior. We have already seen that in the first three verses of Hebrews. Then beginning in verses 4-14 the Holy Spirit teaches us that Jesus Christ is superior to angels.

A. The Biblical View of Angels

Man is a wonderful creation, higher than plants, animals, and any other material creation in this world. But there are created beings even higher than man—angels. Hebrews 2:9 indicates that angels are higher than humans because it says that when Jesus became a man, He "was made a little lower than the angels." After the fall of the rebellious angels under Lucifer, the angels in heaven were no longer subject to sin. These angels are holy, powerful, and wise. They do not suffer the same infirmities as men. They are special beings created by God before He created men. They were in the heavens observing when God created the world. They were made higher than men, at least higher than fallen men.

1. Their appearance

Angels are spirit beings, yet they have some kind of form.

They are even capable of appearing in a human form. Hebrews 13:2 says, "Be not forgetful to entertain strangers; for thereby some have entertained angels unawares." They can also appear in other forms. For example, Matthew 28:3-4 describes an angel who appeared at the scene of Christ's resurrection, sitting on the stone that had been rolled away: "His countenance was like lightning, and his raiment white as snow; and for fear of him the keepers did shake, and became as dead men." This angel appeared in a dazzling, brilliant glory. So when we say that angels are spirits, we do not necessarily mean they have no form. They have a form that can manifest itself as human or in another way.

2. Their creation

All the angels were created simultaneously (Col. 1:16-17). They are unable to procreate (Matt. 22:28-30). God made them all with unique identities. Each angel is a direct creation of God standing in an immediate personal relationship to the Creator who made him.

The Old Testament assumes the existence of angels. There are 108 references in the Old Testament to angels and 165 in the New Testament. There's no doubt that angels exist and that the Old Testament saints were well aware of it.

3. Their attributes

a) Intelligence

Angels render intelligent worship and service to God. That's why they were created—to render service to God of a special nature.

b) Emotion

The Bible says that angels rejoice when sinners are saved (Luke 15:10).

c) Speech

Angels can speak. In Galatians 1:8 the apostle Paul says, "But though we, or an angel from heaven, preach any other gospel unto you . . . "

d) Swiftness

According to Daniel 9:21 angels have incredible speed. Sometimes they are pictured with as many as six wings.

45

4. Their home

According to Mark 13:32 and Jude 6, the unfallen angels have a special abode in heaven. God lives in the third heaven (Deut. 10:14; cf. 2 Cor. 12:2). The second heaven is the universe. The first heaven is the atmosphere of the earth. Are there beings in other parts of the universe? Yes, but they are not beings from other planets; they are angelic beings who inhabit the universe.

5. Their number

The number of angels has not changed since they were originally created, although a great number of them have fallen. So they are not subject to death. Nowhere does Scripture indicate that they can die or be made extinct. They do not decrease or increase. Angels are countless ages older than men, and evidently trillions of them exist. Even after numberless hosts of them fell with Satan, there still remain many holy angels. For example, in Daniel 7:10, Daniel says, "A thousand thousands ministered unto him, and ten thousand times ten thousand stood before him." Revelation 5:11 says, "The number of them was ten thousand times ten thousand, and thousands of thousands."

6. Their power

Angels are more powerful than men, and men must call on divine power to deal with them, especially the fallen ones. Ephesians 6:10-11 says, "Be strong in the Lord, and in the power of his might. . . . For we wrestle not against flesh and blood, but against [fallen angels]."

7. Their organization

Angels are highly organized. Their various ranks are referred to as thrones, dominions, principalities, powers, and authorities (Eph. 6:12; Col. 1:16). Some of the special classes of angels are cherubim, seraphim, and those described as living creatures. Some have names: Lucifer, Michael, and Gabriel. Lucifer is the name Satan had before he fell. Michael is the head of the armies of heaven.

8. Their ministry

Angels are seen in Scripture as spectators at all redemptive events. They minister to God and do His bidding. For example, they ministered to Christ in His humiliation. At the conclusion of His temptation, the Bible says that angels came and ministered to Him (Matt. 4:11). They also minister to the saved by watching over the church and the preacher. They assist God in answering prayer, delivering the saints from danger, encouraging them, and protecting children. In addition, they minister to the unsaved by announcing judgment and carrying it out.

B. The Jewish View of Angels

The Jewish people at the time Hebrews was written had a different view of angels. Many of their views had begun to wander from the basic Old Testament context because of Talmudic writings and rabbinical ideas. The writer of Hebrews had to write this epistle not only with the true biblical view of angels in mind, but also with the exalted Jewish concept of angels as a problem to overcome.

1. Mediated between God and man

The Jews believed that angels were important to the Old Covenant. They had always esteemed angels as the highest beings next to God. They believed angels were the mediators between men and God. For example, they thought that angels surrounded God. They believed angels were the instruments who brought God's Word and worked God's will in the universe and among men. They were thought of as ethereal creatures made of a fiery substance like blazing light—and that analysis may not be far from wrong. They believed that angels were created, that they did not eat or drink, and that they did not procreate.

2. Acted as God's senate

The Jews also believed that angels were God's senate and that God never did anything without first asking the angels. When Genesis 1:26 says, "Let us make man in our image," they believe God was speaking of His angelic senate in the word *us*. Some believed that angels objected to the creation of men and were annihilated for their objection. Others believed angels objected to the giving of the law and attacked Moses on his way up Mount Sinai.

3. Were assigned special tasks

Angels were given names by the Jews. They believed there was a group of "presence angels" who stayed in the presence of God at all times. They were given names such as Raphael, Yuriel, Phanuel, Gabriel, and Michael. *El* was one name for God that was added on at the end of every name. It was believed that there were two hundred angels who controlled the movements of the stars and kept things on course. They believed there was a calendar angel who controlled the never-ending succession of days, months, and years. They believed that there was one mighty angel who took care of the seas, one who took care of frost, one for dew, rain, snow, hail, thunder, lightning, and so on. There were also thought to be angels who were the wardens of hell and the torturers of the damned. They believed that recording angels wrote down every word that every man spoke. They also believed there was an angel of death. And they believed that there was a guardian angel for every nation and every child. There were so many angels that one rabbi said every blade of grass has its angel.

I've given you a backdrop of angels both from the viewpoint of Scripture and from the Jewish people. But one more thing needs to be noted because it has particular significance to the section of Hebrews written in reference to angels.

4.  Gave the Old Testament to Israel

The Jews knew that the Old Covenant and Old Testament were brought to them from God by angels. That belief above any other exalted the angels in the minds of the children of Israel. They believed that angels were the mediators of their covenant with God, and that they continued that ministry all the time.

*a)* The proof

(1) Acts 7:51-53—The following is an excerpt from Stephen's indictment of Israel: "Ye stiff-necked and uncircumcised in heart and ears, ye do always resist the Holy Spirit; as your fathers did, so do ye. Which of the prophets have not your fathers persecuted? And they have slain them who showed before of the coming of the Just One, of whom ye have been now the betrayers and murderers; who have received the law by the disposition of angels, and have not kept it."

(2) Galatians 3:19—"Wherefore, then, serveth the law? It was added because of transgressions, till the seed should come to whom the promise was

made; and it was ordained by angels in the hand of a mediator."

The Old Covenant was brought to men and maintained by angelic mediation. The angels ministered between God and men to carry on the work of the Old Covenant. The Jews knew that and consequently had the highest regard for angels.

*b)* The perversion

Some Jews exalted angels to such a degree that they actually began to worship them. This activity developed into a heresy known as Gnosticism, which reduced Jesus Christ to an angel. The Colossian church had been flirting with Gnosticism when Paul wrote, "Let no man beguile you of your reward in a voluntary humility and worshiping of angels" (Col. 2:18).

Angels were supremely exalted in the Jewish mind. So if the writer of Hebrews is to present to the Hebrews that Christ is the mediator of a better covenant, then he will have to show that Christ is better than angels. That becomes his purpose in Hebrews 1:4-14. He shows that Christ, the bearer of the New Covenant is a better mediator than the mediators of the Old Covenant, who were angels. Therefore, Christ must be better than angels. The writer sets out to prove that by using seven Old Testament passages to verify it.

## The First Translation

If you were to compare the quotations of the seven Old Testament passages in Hebrews 1:4-14 with the same passages in the Old Testament, you would find that they are not quoted exactly— there is slight variation. The reason is this: By the time the epistle of Hebrews was written, there existed a book called the Septuagint, the Greek translation of the Hebrew text. Near the time of Christ there existed such a tremendous number of Greek-speaking Jews, that seventy scholars translated the Hebrew text into Greek. Evidently, the writer of Hebrews was influenced by Greek culture because when he quoted the Old Testament, he invariably used the Septuagint as his source. Consequently, it varies slightly from the Hebrew translation but not in truth or in fact. Where there is some difference, it is not a difference in meaning, only in a phrase or in word choice. One of the reasons many don't believe Paul was the writer of Hebrews is that he usually quoted the Old Testament from the Hebrew text.

## Effective Jewish Evangelism

The writer of Hebrews uses the Old Testament wisely and deftly to show the Jews that Christ is a better mediator, and that's what makes the argument powerful. Were we to try to use the New Testament to prove to Israel that Christ is a better mediator, they would say, "We don't accept the New Testament." So the writer says, "Let me prove it to you from your own Scriptures." We will see the tremendous power that is in this kind of argument.

The text for this lesson is the first part of Hebrews 1:4, "Being made so much better than the angels." That's the proposition the writer seeks to prove. Who is better than the angels? Jesus Christ, who is the subject of verses 1-3. From verses 4-14 the writer goes on to prove that Christ is better than angels.

## In What Sense Was Christ Made Better Than the Angels?

Many cults and unorthodox religious organizations deny the deity of Christ on the basis of Hebrews 1:4. They claim that Christ was not God but a created being. When verse 4 says, "Being made so much better than the angels," they say, "See, Christ was made." But the Greek word used there for "made" is not *poieō*, which means, "to make" or "create"; it is *ginomai*, which means, "to become." Jesus Christ has always existed, but He became better than the angels in His exaltation, inferring at one time that He had been lower than the angels (Heb. 2:9). Specifically, in Hebrews 1:4 the writer is referring to Christ as God's Son. Christ as a man became lower than angels. But as a result of His faithful obedience and the wonderful work He accomplished as a Son, He was exalted above the angels, which is where He had been before. But this time He was exalted as the Son. Christ did not become the Son of God until His incarnation. He was not the Son of God in eternity past; He was God as the second person of the Trinity. For a while He was lower than the angels, faithfully accomplishing God's work; He became better than the angels as the exalted Son.

## Lesson

In what ways was Jesus better than the angels? Five ways: His title, His worship, His nature, His eternity, and His destiny.

I. HIS TITLE (vv. 4-5)

"Being made [becoming] so much better than the angels, as He hath by inheritance obtained a more excellent name than they. For unto which of the angels said he [God] at any time, Thou art my Son, this day have I begotten thee? And again, I will be to him a Father, and he shall be to me a Son?"

A. The Establishment of Sonship

The Holy Spirit says that Jesus is better than angels because He has a better name. To what angel did God ever say, "Thou art my Son, this day have I begotten thee?" To what angel did God ever say, "I will be a Father to You, and You will be a Son to Me?" The answer is: none. The angels are ministers and messengers, but Christ was the Son. That's a great difference. So Christ obtained a more excellent name, or title, than angels.

In our culture the names we pick for our children don't have much connection with the child's character. In the Bible, God chose specific names that had to do with some aspect of individuals' lives. Frequently, the name spoke of an inward reality. Jesus Christ was given a name that is above every name (Phil. 2:9), including angels.

B. The Prophecies of Sonship

The writer quotes two Old Testament passages to show that Jesus has a better name than angels. Hebrews 1:5 quotes Psalm 2:7: "Unto which of the angels said he at any time, Thou art my Son, this day have I begotten thee?" Then again in verse 5 he says, "I will be to him a Father, and he shall be to me a Son." That's a quote from 2 Samuel 7:14, where David had been given a prophecy that he would have a great son. Which angel has ever been called a Son? None. As Christians, we are collectively called "sons of God" or "children of God"; the angels are likewise in the sense that God created them. But no one angel is ever called the "Son of God." Neither has God said to an angel, "This day have I begotten thee." God says, "I have a Son who has a greater name." The Old Testament predicted that a Son was going to come. Psalm 2:7 says, "Thou art my Son; this day have I begotten thee." Second Samuel 7:14 also predicts the coming of the Son: "I will be his father, and he shall be my son."

## C. The Time of Sonship

Did you know that when 2 Samuel was written, Jesus Christ was not the Son of God? Why? The title *Son* refers to Jesus Christ in His incarnation. Christ did not become the Son until He was begotten into time. Prior to His incarnation, He was the eternal God. God as Father and Jesus as the Son is God's analogy to help us understand the relationship between the first and second Persons of the Trinity. The writer of Hebrews is presenting to the Jewish reader that Christ incarnate is God. So He speaks of Him in His incarnate title.

Nothing in the Bible speaks of the eternal Sonship of Christ. When the writer refers to Christ's eternality in verse 8 he says, "But unto the Son he saith, Thy throne, O God, is forever and ever." Note that he uses the title *God*. When he's talking about Christ's incarnation, however, he uses the title Son.

1. It is excellent

   Why does verse 4 say, "As he hath by inheritance obtained a more excellent name than they"? Didn't Christ always have a more excellent name? Yes, but He obtained another one. He was always God, but He became the Son, which is more excellent than servant. He did not always have the title Son. Eternally Christ is God, but He is Son in His incarnation.

2. It is not eternal

   There are people who believe that Jesus is a Son to God, and therefore eternally inferior to God. But He never became a Son until His incarnation. Before that He was the eternal God. It is incorrect to say that Jesus Christ is inferior to God because He has the title of Son. He acquired that title when He came into the world in His incarnation. Don't let anyone tell you that Christ is the eternal Son—always subservient and less than God—because He is not. Christ's Sonship is only an analogy to allow the human mind to comprehend His willing submission to the Father for the sake of our redemption. The phrase "this day" in Hebrews 1:5 shows that Christ's Sonship began at a point in time, not in eternity. Christ is a Son in a human sense because His life was conceived in this world.

   The part of verse 5 that says, "I will be to him a Father, and he shall be to me a Son" emphasizes the future. Let

52

me illustrate that in John 1:14, which refers to a time before Jesus had been born into the world. Was Christ a Son before He was born into the world? No. John was careful to make the distinction in verse 14: "The Word [John's term for Christ] was made flesh." John didn't refer to Christ as the Son until He was made flesh. So there is no justification for saying that Jesus Christ is eternally subservient to God or less than God.

D. The Fullness of Sonship

There are two basic areas in which Christ is a Son.

1. His virgin birth

Christ was not a Son until He came into this world through the virgin birth.

a) Luke 1:35—"The angel answered, and said unto her [Mary], The Holy Spirit shall come upon thee, and the power of the Highest shall overshadow thee; therefore also that holy thing which shall be born of thee shall be called the Son of God." Christ was not called the Son of God until He was born. Verse 32 says, "He shall be great, and shall be called the Son of the Highest."

b) Luke 3:22—At Christ's baptism "the Holy Spirit descended in a bodily shape like a dove upon him, and a voice came from heaven, which said, Thou art my beloved Son." After Christ's incarnation, God said, "This is My Son!" Prior to that, God had never referred to Christ in that way.

Since the phrase "this day" in Hebrews 1:5 could not refer to eternal Sonship, it must refer to a point in time. Luke 2:11 uses the phrase "for unto you is born this day." The Son was born at a point in time. Christ's Sonship began with His virgin birth. Prior to that He was eternal God in the Godhead with the other members of the Trinity.

2. His resurrection

Jesus' Sonship came to full bloom in His resurrection. He is a Son not only because He was begotten of a virgin but also because He was begotten again from the dead. You and I become sons of God in the fullest sense not by being born once but by being born twice (John 3:3). The same was true of Jesus.

*a)* Romans 1:3-4—"Concerning His Son, Jesus Christ our Lord, who was made of the seed of David according to the flesh, and declared to be the Son of God with power, according to the spirit of holiness, by the resurrection from the dead." Christ was made a Son in birth, and He was declared to be a Son in resurrection. The fullness of His Sonship is in His twin birth.

*b)* Acts 13:33—This verse also quotes Psalm 2:7, as does Hebrews 1:5: "God hath fulfilled the same unto us their children, in that he hath raised up Jesus again; as it is also written in the second psalm, Thou art my Son, this day have I begotten Thee." That tells us conclusively that Psalm 2:7 is related to the resurrection.

Jesus is a Son in resurrection. In the Old Testament it was prophesied that He would come as a Son. In the New Testament He came as a Son in His virgin birth and was declared to be the Son by His resurrection from the dead. Don't ever get trapped into the heresy of those who propagate that Jesus Christ is eternally subservient to God. He set aside what was rightfully His and humbled Himself to become a Son for our sake.

Angels are the most excellent of all creatures, but if Christ has a more excellent name than they, He must have the most excellent name. So the writer of Hebrews tells his readers from their own Scriptures that Jesus Christ is greater than angels because He obtained a greater name.

II. HIS WORSHIP (v. 6)

"And again, when he bringeth in the first-begotten into the world, he saith, And let all the angels of God worship him."

Even though Jesus Christ humbled Himself and was made lower than the angels for a time, angels are still to worship Him. If angels are to worship Him, then He must be greater than they. Therefore His covenant is greater than the one they brought—Christianity is greater than Judaism. Hebrews 1:6 quotes Psalm 97:7. The psalmist was saying that all angels were to worship the Lord's Christ. The Jews should not have been surprised at that because it came right out of their own Scripture.

Didn't the angels always worship Christ? Yes. They worshiped Him throughout all the time of their existence prior to His

54

incarnation, only they worshiped Him as God. But then they were called to worship Him as the Son. This Son who became a man is higher than angels because He is the very God that angels have always worshiped. Did you know it is an absolute sin and violation of all God's laws to worship anyone but God? And if God is saying that all the angels worship the Son, then the Son must be God. Christ is not only the God of eternity but also the Son of humanity. In His incarnate Person, even as in His eternal Person, Christ is to be worshiped.

A. His Position

1. Defined

Verse 6 says that Christ is the "first-begotten." Many people use this word as their proof text that Jesus is a created being. But they don't understand that the word "first-begotten" does not have anything to do with time but position. Colossians 1:15 says Christ "is the image of the invisible God, the first-born of all creation." They also try to use that as a proof text. They claim Colossians 1:15 proves that Christ was created. But the Greek word for "first-begotten" and "firstborn" is *prōtotokos*, which means "the chief one." Christ was not begotten; He is the chief, the sovereign of everything. That term was connected with the concept of the firstborn because the eldest son was usually the heir to everything—the chief of the father's estate. *Prōtotokos* then came to mean, "one with all the dignity and honor who stood as the chief one." Jesus Christ is the *prōtotokos*. And that refers to His right and authority, not to His time of birth.

There were two brothers in the Old Testament named Jacob and Esau. Esau was the oldest, but Jacob was the *prōtotokos*. Genesis 49:3 describes the character of Jacob's *prōtotokos*: "Reuben, thou art my first-born, my might, and the beginning of my strength, the excellence of dignity, and the excellency of power." What does *prōtotokos* mean? Might, strength, dignity, and power. So it is not a word of time; it is a word of authority. Jesus Christ is the *prōtotokos* in the sense that He has the right to rule.

2. Dignified

Colossians 1:18 says Christ "is the head of the body, the church; who is the beginning, the first-born from the dead." That verse indicates Jesus as the firstborn from the dead. Now, had anyone been resurrected before Jesus? Yes—Lazarus and the other people Jesus resurrected during His earthly life, the Old Testament saints who were raised at the crucifixion, and all others who were raised from the dead before Jesus as recorded in the Old Testiment. Yet Colossians 1:18 says He was the firstborn from the dead. That means Christ was the chief One of all who had ever been raised. The word *firstborn* can't refer to time or else the verse would be a lie. *Prōtotokos* means that Christ is the main One, the most honored One, the most dignified One, the highest One, and the most powerful One. Of all those who were resurrected, Jesus is the greatest. The title refers to Christ's glory and dignity, not to the concept of being created before anything else was created.

B.  His Return

The existence of the word *again* in Hebrews 1:6 has caused commentators, including myself, many problems: "And *again*, when He bringeth in the [*prōtotokos*] into the world, He saith, And let all the angels of God worship Him" (emphasis added).

1.  The destination of Christ

    Before we can understand the word *again* here, we need to define what is meant by the word *world*. The common Greek word for "world" (*kosmos*), which refers to the whole universe, is not used here. The Greek word that is used is *oikoumenē*, which means, "the inhabited earth." Christ was not the first to be born on earth, yet He is the firstborn— the chief One, the dignified One—who came to an already inhabited earth.

2.  The day of return

    We need to look at verse 6 in the order of the Greek text: "And *when* again He brings in the [*prōtotokos*] into the world" (emphasis added). When is the "again" going to take place? At the second coming. God already brought Christ into the world once as Son, and He's going to bring Him again in the future in blazing glory.

3.  The desire of the angels

    It is at the second coming that the fullness of the prophecy in verse 6 comes to pass: "Let all the angels of God worship Him." At present, the angels don't fully understand the whole picture of God's redemptive plan. First Peter 1:11-12 presents the picture of the Old Testament prophets, who wrote down what God told them and then read what they wrote to determine what it meant. They were inspired by the Holy Spirit but in many cases didn't understand it, "searching what, or what manner of time the Spirit of Christ who was in them did signify, when he testified beforehand the sufferings of Christ, and the glory that should follow. Unto whom it was revealed that, not unto themselves but unto us they did minister the things which are now reported unto you by them that have preached the gospel unto you with the Holy Spirit sent down from heaven." The things the prophets couldn't understand were not to be understood until Christ came, the gospel was preached, and the Spirit was made manifest. Verse 12 continues, "Which things the angels desire to look into." Even the angels don't understand all God's revelation as yet. Perhaps the "presence angels" around God's throne understand, but the vast angelic hosts are evidently not yet able to discern everything. They are not omniscient. It is not until God brings the *prōtotokos* into the world that the angels will be able to give full and complete worship.

4. The delight of worship

I believe that the angels around the throne worship God now, and I also believe that there might be angels who worship the Son, but if I read my Bible right, the angels are still trying to figure out things they don't understand. But once the time comes for Jesus to return, how are the angels going to react? In Revelation 5:11-12 the apostle John says, "I beheld, and I heard the voice of many angels round about the throne and the living creatures and the elders, and the number of them was ten thousand times ten thousand, and thousands of thousands, saying with a loud voice, Worthy is the Lamb that was slain to receive power, and riches, and wisdom, and strength, and honor, and glory, and blessing." That is what angelic worship will be like when Christ comes again to take the earth.

In Revelation 5:1, the Father is pictured holding the title deed to the earth, a scroll, and an angel says, "Who is worthy to open the scroll, and to loose its seals?" (v. 2). The apostle John begins crying in verse 4 because no one was found to open the scroll. But in verse 5 one of the elders says, "Weep not; behold, the Lion of the tribe of

Judah, the Root of David, hath prevailed to open the scroll, and to loose its seven seals." Jesus Christ, the Lamb, takes the scroll. As He is about to unroll the judgments and take possession of the earth, the angels say, "Oh, it's all clear now!" Praises burst forth from millions of angels in heaven. Verses 13-14 says, "Every creature that is in heaven, and on the earth, and under the earth, and such as are in the sea, and all that are in them, heard I saying, Blessing, and honor, and glory, and power be unto him that sitteth upon the throne, and unto the Lamb forever and ever. And the four living creatures said, Amen. And the four and twenty elders fell down and worshiped him that liveth forever and ever."

It is at the second coming that Christ is revealed in His full glory as the Son—the *prōtotokos*. Even the angels will understand it all when they see Him return as King of kings and Lord of lords. Christ is greater than angels because God commands angels to worship Him. And if God commanded the angels to worship His Son, then His Son must be God.

## Focusing on the Facts

1. How do we know that angels are higher created beings than humans (see p. 44)?
2. What kind of form can angels take (see p. 45)?
3. Describe some of the attributes of angels (see p. 45).
4. Describe the ministry of angels (see pp. 46-47).
5. What did the Jewish people believe to be true about angels? Explain (see pp. 47-48).
6. What belief, above any other belief, exalted the angels in the minds of the Jewish people (see p. 48)?
7. What heresy developed as the result of Jews who began to worship angels (see p. 49)?
8. What did the writer of Hebrews use to prove the superiority of Christ over angels (see p. 49)?
9. Why are quotations from the Old Testament in Hebrews 1:4-14 different from the original passages in the Old Testament (see p. 49)?
10. Explain how Christ was made lower than angels (see p. 50).
11. What does the title "Son of God" refer to about Jesus Christ? Explain (see pp. 51-52).
12. Why is it incorrect to say that Jesus Christ is inferior to God because He is called "Son" (see p. 52)?

13. What are the two areas of Christ's life in which He is manifest as the Son (see pp. 53-54)?
14. What does the word *first-begotten* in Hebrews 1:6 refer to? What is the significance of that (see p. 55)?
15. Explain what Colossians 1:18 means (see pp. 55-56).
16. What does the word *again* in Hebrews 1:6 refer to (see p. 56)?
17. What does 1 Peter 1:12 indicate about the angels' understanding of God's redemptive plan (see pp. 56-57)?
18. How will the angels react when Jesus returns (Rev. 5:11-14; see pp. 57-58)?

## Pondering the Principles

1. The writer of Hebrews used seven Old Testament passages to verify Christ's superiority over angels. That is just a sampling of the many times that the writers of the New Testament used the Old Testament to verify God's timeless truths. As an exercise, match the following New Testament passages to the Old Testament passage it quotes:

| | |
|---|---|
| a. Galatians 3:8 | 1. Deuteronomy 8:3 |
| b. Hebrews 8:5 | 2. Psalm 14:1-3 |
| c. Romans 9:15 | 3. Genesis 12:3 |
| d. Matthew 5:43 | 4. Isaiah 40:13 |
| e. Matthew 4:4 | 5. Exodus 25:40 |
| f. Hebrews 13:5 | 6. Leviticus 19:18 |
| g. Romans 11:34 | 7. Exodus 33:19 |
| h. Romans 3:10-12 | 8. Deuteronomy 31:6, 8 |

What truth does each of those passages verify? Thank God for the consistency of His Word. His truths are timeless. As you study the Bible, be aware of the many Old Testament passages that the New Testament writers use to verify God's truths. Use them to share the truth of Christ with Jewish people who do not know that Jesus is the Savior of their own Scriptures.

2. Look up the following verses: Matthew 16:16-17; 28:18-19; John 1:3-4; 5:25-27; 10:30; Philippians 2:10; Colossians 1:17; Hebrews 13:8; Revelation 19:16. What does each of those verses have to say about the deity of Christ? When people bring Christ's deity into question, you need to be able to show them He is God, just as the writer of Hebrews did. To better prepare yourself, do additional study into the deity of Christ. You might find a theology book on the doctrine of Christ to be helpful.

# 4
# Jesus Christ, Superior to Angels— Part 2

## Outline

Introduction
A. The Theme of Scripture
 1. Matthew 5:17
 2. Luke 24:27
 3. Luke 24:44-45
 4. John 5:39
 5. Hebrews 10:7
B. The Transition of Scripture
 1. Its completion
  a) The veil that lingers
  b) The veil that is lifted
 2. Its change
  a) The temporary Old Covenant
   (1) Hebrews 8:13
   (2) Hebrews 10:1
   (3) Hebrews 10:9
   (4) Hebrews 11:40
  b) The eternal New Covenant

Review
 I. His Title (vv. 4-5)
 II. His Worship (v. 6)

Lesson
III. His Nature (vv. 7-9)
 A. The Nature of Angels (v. 7)
  1. Their creation
  2. Their characteristics
   a) Rapid movement
   b) Fierce judgment
    (1) Genesis 19:13-16, 26

61

## Introduction

The book of Hebrews was written to exalt Christ—to show the Jewish reader that Christ is superior to everything and everyone. Our blessed, matchless Christ is the supreme Person of the book of Hebrews, just as He is in all the universe.

  A.  The Theme of Scripture

      Throughout Scripture, the person of Jesus Christ is exalted. He is the theme of the Old Testament as well as the New Testament.

1.  Matthew 5:17—Jesus said, "Think not that I am come to destroy the law, or the prophets; I am not come to destroy, but to fulfill." Christ was the fulfillment of Old Testament truth.

2.  Luke 24:27—Jesus said the following to two disciples on the road to Emmaus: "Beginning at Moses and all the prophets, he expounded unto them, in all the scriptures [the Old Testament] the things concerning himself." The law, the prophets, and the writings make up the Old Testament. So Jesus taught concerning Himself from the Old Testament.

3.  Luke 24:44-45—Jesus said to His disciples, "These are the words which I spoke unto you, while I was yet with you, that all things must be fulfilled, which were written in the law of Moses, and in the prophets, and in the psalms, concerning me. Then opened he their understanding, that they might understand the scriptures." No one, whether he is Jew or Gentile, will ever understand the Old Testament until he understands it in terms of Jesus Christ.

4.  John 5:39—Jesus told the Jewish leaders, "Search the scriptures [the Old Testament]; for in them ye think ye have eternal life; and they are they which testify of me."

5.  Hebrews 10:7—"Then said I [Christ], Lo, I come (in the volume of the book it is written of me)."

The theme of the Old Testament is the Person of Jesus Christ. Although His life is not explained until the New Testament, He is nonetheless the theme and fulfillment of the Old Testament. But Jesus is also the theme of the New Testament. The apostle John said the following was the purpose of writing his gospel, which could well be the purpose of the whole New Testament: "These are written, that ye might believe that Jesus is the Christ, the Son of God; and that believing ye might have life through his name" (John 20:31). Jesus Christ is the theme of both the Old and New Testaments. Consequently, it is no wonder that Jewish people who adhere to the old text have trouble interpreting it. They cannot understand it apart from Christ.

B.  The Transition of Scripture

Whatever the Old Testament concealed of Christ, the New Testament revealed. Whatever the Old Testament contained of Christ, the New Testament explained. Whatever the Old

Testament gave in precept about Christ, the New Testament gives in perfection. Whatever the Old Testament presented of Christ in shadow, the New Testament presents in substance. Whatever the Old Testament presented of Christ in ritual, the New Testament presents in reality. Whatever the Old Testament presented of Christ in picture, the New Testament presents of Christ in Person. What was foretold is fulfilled; prophecy became history.

1. Its completion

   *a)* The veil that lingers

   The New Testament presentation of Jesus Christ closes the meaning of the Old Testament. Second Corinthians 3:14-16 says, "Their minds were blinded; for until this day remaineth the same veil untaken away in the reading of the old testament; which veil is done away in Christ. But even unto this day, when Moses is read, the veil is upon their heart. Nevertheless, when it shall turn to the Lord, the veil shall be taken away." There is no way that anyone will ever understand the Old Testament apart from understanding and knowing Jesus Christ. The veil remains until they turn to Christ. That's why it is so difficult for the majority of Jewish people to understand the Old Testament. In Judaism today there remains only a small group of Orthodox Jews; the great majority have wandered off into liberal Judaism because they cannot adhere to rituals that have no meaning apart from fulfillment.

   *b)* The veil that is lifted

   The writer of Hebrews gives this message to his people: Jesus Christ removes the veil and not only brings understanding of the Old Covenant but also brings a better covenant because it explains the Old. Everything in the Old Testament is not obsolete; there remain basic principles and eternal truths of God. Everything did not pass away, only some things. The forms, types, and rituals passed away because the reality has come. But the principles of morality and God's attitude toward sin remain the same.

2. Its change

   a) The temporary Old Covenant

   Hebrews speaks of the temporary nature of the Old Covenant in the sense of its forms.

   (1) Hebrews 8:13—"A New Covenant, he hath made the first old. Now that which decayeth and groweth old is ready to vanish away." That does not mean everything God said in the Old Testament is no longer true—that you now can covet, murder, or do whatever you want because Old Testament morality is gone. It means that the forms, rituals, types, pictures, and symbols of the Old Testament are no longer necessary because the reality has arrived.

   (2) Hebrews 10:1—"For the law, having a shadow of good things to come and not the very image of the things, can never with those sacrifices which they offered year by year continually make those who come to it perfect." The Old Testament sacrifices couldn't make a man perfect; they were merely pictures of Christ, who alone could bring perfection.

   (3) Hebrews 10:9—"Then said he, Lo, I come to do thy will, O God. He taketh away the first, that he may establish the second." The tendency of the Jewish believers was to receive Christ and then hang onto the rituals of Judaistic symbolism. The writer of Hebrews is saying, "You've got the New, so let go of the Old. You can't mix the two."

   (4) Hebrews 11:40—"God having provided some better thing for us, that they without us should not be made perfect." Perfection was not provided for in the Old Covenant; there was only a picture of it. The perfection came in the better thing—the New Covenant.

   Throughout Hebrews are other statements regarding the change from the Old to the New. For example, the Aaronic priesthood needed to be changed because it was inadequate, and so did the rituals of Israel (7:12). The Old Testament priests were only a shadow of the heavenly Priest, Christ (8:1-5). The sacrifices were abolished (9:12-15). The Old Covenant was not faultless, so it decayed and vanished away (8:7, 13). The

Old Covenant was merely a temporal shadow of things to come.

b) The eternal New Covenant

When we open up the book of Hebrews we see that the New Covenant isn't a shadow at all—it's the real thing. It isn't a picture; it's a Person. It's not the imperfect priesthood; it's the perfect Priest. It's not repeated sacrifices that couldn't alleviate sin; it's the one sacrifice that took care of sin once for all.

In Hebrews, everything is eternal. We read about eternal salvation (5:9), eternal judgment (6:2), eternal redemption (9:12), eternal inheritance (9:15), and an eternal covenant (13:20). The New Covenant is eternal; the Old was temporal and passing away.

The Old Testament principles and morality are still good. The things that are taught about God and man are still valid. But all the ritual and forms are gone because the reality has arrived. The heavenly High Priest has come; you don't need the priests of Judaism. The once-and-for-all sacrifice has been accomplished, so we're to forget the continual sacrifices. Once the reality has come, the ritual, which prefigured it, is no longer needed. The Holy Spirit is saying this to the Hebrew Christian: "Make a total and complete break with Judaistic ritual. You don't need it so don't hang onto any of it." To the unsaved Hebrew He is saying, "Recognize the better covenant. Turn to Jesus Christ and embrace it."

## Substituting Ritual for Reality

Many churches today are ritualistic. But you need to realize that there is no need for excessive symbols, types, and liturgy because the reality in Christ is here. Why would I want to lead you in rituals that symbolize Jesus when I can say, "Let me take you to this verse and show you what it says about Him"? The coming of Christ spelled the end of ritual.

It is tragic that the church today, like the early Hebrew Christians, has hung onto symbolism and rejected the reality. Symbolism is unnecessary. The Lord told us that only two symbols are important: one, the Lord's table, which remembers the cross; and two, baptism, which testifies to our identification with Christ. Apart from those two, no ritual belongs in the church of Jesus Christ. We are not to spend our time in forms and symbols when we have the reality. Many people think they are religious because they practice ritual, but they are substituting ritual for reality and form for a relationship. The tragic thing about those people is that so many of them are lost in the patterns of ritual and have missed the truth. We don't need pictures or illustrations; we have the realization of everything in Jesus Christ because He is the key Person in the New Covenant. Once He arrived, the rituals, types, and pictures were replaced by the reality.

## Review

To prove that the New Testament is better than the Old, the writer of Hebrews must prove that Jesus is better than anyone or anything attached to the Old Covenant. If it's a better covenant, it must have a better mediator. So the book of Hebrews attempts to prove that Jesus Christ is superior to everything and everyone connected to the Old Covenant. So far we have learned that the Old Covenant was mediated to men by angels, and that the Jewish people revered and esteemed angels higher than any other created being. So if the writer is to show that Jesus is a better mediator with a better covenant, he must prove that Jesus is better than angels.

The proposition of Hebrews 1:4-14 is in verse 4: "Being made so much better than the angels." For a short time Jesus became lower than the angels (in His incarnation), but He was then exalted above them once more. Jesus was made lower in the sense that he became a man; He was not lower in the sense of His deity. The writer gives us five ways that Jesus is better than angels: His title, His worship, His nature, His eternity, and His destiny.

I. HIS TITLE (vv. 4-5; see pp. 51-54)

### The Son or a son?

The name Son belongs to Jesus in His incarnation. When Christ appeared in the Old Testament, He was not called Son; He was called "the angel of the Lord." In Daniel 3:25, when the king looked into the fiery furnace, he saw Shadrach, Meshach, Abednego, and one "like the Son of God" (KJV*). But any of the new translations have corrected it to say what it ought to say: like *a son* of the gods" (emphasis added). That was a pagan's comment indicating that whoever the fourth person was, he looked like something from another world. But it is not the title of

*King James Version.

Jesus Christ. "The Son of God" is a New Testament title referring to Christ in His incarnation. He became a Son in His virgin birth and in His resurrection.

II. HIS WORSHIP (v. 6; see pp. 54-58)

**Lesson**

III. HIS NATURE (vv. 7-9)

Here the Holy Spirit shows the basic difference in the nature of angels and of the Son, Jesus Christ.

A. The Nature of Angels (v. 7)

"And of the angels he saith, Who maketh his angels spirits, and his ministers a flame of fire."

1. Their creation

The Greek word for "maketh" is *poieō*, which means "to create." The antecedent of "who" is Christ. So who created angels? Christ. And if Christ created angels, He must be greater than they are. Hebrews 1:2 says, "By his Son, whom he hath appointed heir of all things, by whom also he made the worlds [Gk., *aiōnas*]." Christ made the entire universe. John 1:3 says that nothing was created without Him. Jesus made the angels, so we know they are created beings.

Hebrews 1:7 also indicates that the angels are Christ's angels—they are His possession. Verse 7 is a quote from Psalm 104:4. So again the writer of Hebrews uses the Old Testament to verify the superiority of Christ over angels.

2. Their characteristics

*a)* Rapid movement

The world *spirits* can also mean "wind." Angels are spirits, but because of the comparison with fire, we will interpret it as "winds." Why would angels be called winds? Because of their invisible, powerful, and rapid movement.

*b)* Fierce judgment

Verse 7 also calls angels "flames of fire." Angels not only move rapidly to carry out God's bidding but also are flames of fire. The phrase "flame of fire" fits in connection with divine judgment. So we see that angels are God's executioners. They mete out judgment on the earth.

(1) Genesis 19:13-16, 26—This is a familiar passage dealing with the prelude to the destruction of Sodom: "We [two angels] will destroy this place, because the cry of them has become great before the face of the Lord; and the Lord hath sent us to destroy it. And Lot went out, and spoke unto his sons-in-law, who married his daughters, and said, Up, get you out of this place; for the Lord will destroy this city. But he seemed as one that mocked unto his sons-in-law. And when the morning arose, then the angels hastened Lot, saying, Arise, take thy wife, and thy two daughters, which are here; lest thou be consumed in the iniquity of the city. And while he lingered, the men [angels in the form of men] laid hold upon his hand, and upon the hand of his wife, and upon the hand of his two daughters, the Lord being merciful unto him: and they brought him forth, and set him outside of the city" (vv. 13-16). Those angels were sent to destroy Sodom, and they had to take Lot and his family by force out of the city. Lot's wife was warned not to look back, but she did and was turned into a pillar of salt (v. 26). So angels appear in Genesis 19 as executioners.

(2) Psalm 78:49—"Be cast upon them the fierceness of his anger, wrath, and indignation, and trouble, by sending evil angels among them." I don't believe that "evil angels" refers to demons; I believe they are angels of judgment. God sent his angels of judgment to bring anger, wrath, indignation, and trouble.

(3) Matthew 13:41-42—"The Son of man shall send forth his angels, and they shall gather out of his kingdom all things that offend, and them who do iniquity, and shall cast them into a furnace of fire; there shall be wailing and gnashing of teeth." In the Great Judgment angels are the executioners.

In Hebrews 1:7 we see that angels are winds—they are powerful, swift, and invisible—and they are also agents of judgment. But most significantly, they are beings created by

Jesus Christ and possessed by Him. Angels are created servants. They do not operate on their own initiative but on the direction of God and Christ.

B. The Nature of Christ (vv. 8-9)

What is the difference between the nature of angels and the nature of Christ?

1. In eternity (v. 8)

   a) The proof of deity (v. 8a)

   "But unto the Son he saith, Thy throne, O God, is forever and ever."

   The difference between angels and the Son is that the Son is the eternal God. People who say Jesus was just a man, an angel, a prophet, or some inferior god are wrong and bring upon themselves the curse of God. Jesus is God. The Father acknowledges the Son as God.

   I believe verse 8 supplies us with one of the most powerful, clear, emphatic, and irrefutable proofs of the deity of Christ in the Bible. And there are many verses that corroborate it.

   (1) John 5:18—"The Jews sought the more to kill him, because he not only had broken the sabbath, but said also that God was his Father, making himself equal with God." Jesus all along claimed equality with God.

   (2) John 10:30, 33—Jesus said, "I and my Father are one. . . . The Jews answered him, saying, For a good work we stone thee not, but for blasphemy; and because that thou, being a man, makest thyself God." The Jews understood Christ's claim, and that's more than I can say for a lot of so-called Bible scholars.

   (3) Romans 9:5—This verse discusses Israel "whose are the fathers, and of whom, as concerning the flesh, Christ came, who is over all, God blessed forever." The King James translators put a comma before God instead of after. The verse should say, "Who is over all God, blessed forever."

   (4) 1 Timothy 3:16—"Without controversy great is the mystery of godliness: God was manifest in the flesh, justified in the Spirit, seen of angels,

70

preached unto the nations, believed on in the world, received up into glory."

(5) Titus 2:13—We're to be "looking for that blessed hope, and the glorious appearing of the great God and our Savior, Jesus Christ."

(6) 1 John 5:20—"We know that the Son of God is come, and hath given us an understanding, that we may know him that is true; and we are in him that is true, even in his Son Jesus Christ. This is the true God."

b) The rule of eternity (v. 8b)

"A sceptre of righteousness is the sceptre of thy kingdom."

The sceptre is the symbol of rule. Jesus Christ rules eternity. He is the eternal King with an eternal kingdom and a sceptre of righteousness. He rules justly and righteously.

2. In His incarnation (v. 9)

"Thou hast loved righteousness, and hated iniquity; therefore, God, even thy God, hath anointed thee with the oil of gladness above thy fellows."

a) His motives (v. 9a)

"Thou has loved righteousness, and hated iniquity."

Those words reveal not only the actions of Jesus but also His motives.

(1) He loves righteousness

Christ doesn't just do righteous things; He actually loves righteousness itself. How many times have we obeyed without joy, in an attitude of unwilling condescension?

(a) James 1:17—"Every good gift and every perfect gift is from above, and cometh down from the Father of lights, with whom is no variableness, neither shadow of turning."

(b) 1 John 1:5—"This, then, is the message which we have heard of him, and declare unto you, that God is light, and in him is no darkness at all." God never varies. He's total light—perfect righteousness. If Jesus is God, then He must love righteousness and hate iniquity. And He does. Everything Jesus did sprung from His love for righteousness.

(c) Psalm 119:97—"Oh, how I love thy law! It is my meditation all the day."

(2) He hates iniquity

Since Jesus Christ loves righteousness, He also hates iniquity. The word translated "iniquity" in verse 9 is *anomia* in the Greek text and means "lawlessness." Since Christ loves what is right, He must hate what is wrong. The two are inseparable. One cannot exist without the other. You cannot truthfully say, "I love righteousness, but I also like sin." Yet most of us act that way. When there is true love for God, there will be true love for righteousness and total hatred of sin. Jesus hated sin. You see it in His temptation, His cleansing of the Temple, and His death on the cross. The more you and I become conformed to Jesus Christ, the more we will love righteousness and hate sin. You can determine how close you are to being conformed to Christ by your attitude toward righteousness and sin. Unfortunately, most Christians would have to agree that although they love righteousness, they also love sin to a degree.

b) His majesty (v. 9b)

"God, even thy God, hath anointed thee with the oil of gladness above thy fellows."

Some commentators think the word *fellows* refers to men, but that's not the issue of the passage. The Greek word for "fellows" refers to an association—an association of messengers. Angels are God's messengers, but Christ is a greater messenger. Christ is exalted above the angels.

(1) The meaning of Christ's anointment

Verse 9 says that God anointed Christ. The only one who was ever anointed was the king. That was God's design in the Old Testament. When Jesus Christ was anointed, that indicated He was greater than angels. In Acts 10:38, Peter tells Cornelius how God anointed Jesus of Nazareth.

72

The Old Testament anticipates God's anointed in Psalm 2:2. David is the type of the Lord's anointed. The word in the Old Testament for the coming Redeemer was the "Anointed One," which is transliterated "Messiah." The word *Christ* also means "Anointed One."

(2) The time of Christ's anointment

When was Christ anointed? When He went to heaven after His resurrection. It was at that time that the Father exalted Him and gave Him a name above every name (Phil. 2:9). He assumed His kingship at His ascension. He hasn't brought all His kingdom together yet, but someday soon He will.

Jesus has a greater nature than angels. Hebrews 1:8-9 establish Christ's deity and His exalted position. It mentions His kingship. It reveals the excellence of His rule. It shows the perfection of His incarnate character. It displays His willing submission to God. It announces His coronation. And it reveals His preeminence.

IV. HIS ETERNITY (vv. 10-12)

The Holy Spirit quotes Psalm 102:25-27 to show that Christ is better because He is the eternal Creator.

A. The Creation (v. 10)

"And, Thou, Lord, in the beginning hast laid the foundation of the earth; and the heavens are the works of thine hands."

To create in the beginning, Christ must have been before the beginning. Thus He is without beginning. John 1:1 says, "In the beginning was the Word." If Christ laid the foundation of the earth and created the heavens, then He must have populated it with angels. So He is the creator of angels.

B. The Contrast (vv. 11-12)

"They shall perish [the heavens and the earth], but thou remainest; and they all shall become old as doth a garment, and as a vesture shalt thou fold them up, and they shall be changed; but thou art the same, and thy years shall not fail."

Jesus is no creature. He is eternal. He is immutable, which means that He never changes. Hebrews 13:8 says, "Jesus Christ, the same yesterday, and today, and forever." The writer contrasts the passing of the temporal with the eternal.

The things that look so permanent will fold up someday. In 2 Peter 3:4, after being warned of God's judgment, the people say, "All things continue as they were from the beginning of the creation." Don't you believe it! Hebrews 1:11 says, "They shall perish, but thou remainest; and they all shall become old as doth the garment." When clothes get old, you throw them away. Then verse 12 says, "And as a vesture shalt thou fold them up." Did you know that God is going to roll up the heavens?

1. Revelation 6:14—"The heaven departed as a scroll when it is rolled together; and every mountain and island were moved out of their places." During the time of the Tribulation, the heavens, as if stretched to all corners, rolls right up like a scroll. That's what's going to happen to the sky. The stars are going to fall to the earth. Every island and every mountain will be moved out of their places. The whole world is going to fall apart.

2. Revelation 8:7-10, 12-13—"The first angel sounded, and there followed hail and fire mixed with blood, and they were cast upon the earth; and the third part of trees was burnt up, and all green grass was burnt up. And the second angel sounded, and, as it were, a great mountain burning with fire was cast into the sea; and the third part of the sea became blood; and the third part of the creatures which were in the sea, and had life, died; and the third part of the ships were destroyed. And the third angel sounded, and there fell a great star from heaven, burning as though it were a lamp, and it fell upon the third part of the rivers, and upon the fountains of waters. . . . And the fourth angel sounded, and the third part of the sun was smitten, and the third part of the moon, and the third part of the stars, so that the third part of them was darkened, and the day shown not for a third part of it, and the night likewise" (vv. 7-10, 12). Verse 13 indicates that the next trumpet would be even worse. Our earth and sky, as we know it, is headed for a collapse. When the Bible says, "They shall perish," that's exactly what will happen.

Although creation will perish, Jesus will not. He will create a new heaven and a new earth. Men, worlds, and stars are subject to decay. But Jesus Christ never changes, and He is never subject to change.

V. HIS DESTINY (vv. 13-14)

The destiny of Jesus is greater than angels. The writer closes with

74

the seventh Old Testament quote from Psalm 110:1. First he presents the destiny of Christ and then the destiny of angels.

A. The Destiny of Christ (v. 13)

"But to which of the angels said he at any time, Sit on my right hand, until I make thine enemies thy footstool?"

1. An eternal reign

    *a*) The theology

    The destiny of Jesus Christ is that ultimately everything in the universe will be subject to Him.

        (1) Philippians 2:10—"At the name of Jesus every knee should bow, of things in heaven, and things in earth, and things under the earth." According to God's plan, Jesus Christ is destined to be the ruler of the universe and everything that inhabits it.

        (2) 1 Corinthians 15:23-28—"Every man in his own order: Christ the first fruits; afterward they that are Christ's at his coming. Then cometh the end, when he shall have delivered up the kingdom to God, even the Father, when he shall have put down all rule and all authority and power. For he must reign, till he hath put all enemies under his feet. The last enemy that shall be destroyed is death. For he hath put all things under his feet. . . . And when all things shall be subdued unto him, then shall the Son also himself be subject unto him that put all things under him, that God may be all in all." Only in His Sonship is Christ subordinate to God. Under His feet are placed all the kingdoms, authorities,and powers of the world.

    *b*) The time

    Christ puts everything in subjection under Him when He comes in glory at his second coming. Revelation 19:15-16 says, 'And out of his mouth goeth a sharp sword, that with it he should smite the nations, and he shall rule them with a rod of iron; and he treadeth the winepress of the fierceness and wrath of Almighty God. And he hath on his vesture and on his thigh a name written, KING OF KINGS, AND LORD

75

OF LORDS." The destiny of Jesus Christ is an eternal reign.

2. An eternal rest

Hebrews 1:13 says that Christ sits. There is never any mention in Scripture of angels sitting. Why? Because their work is never done. Fortunately, Christians are able to rest.

*a)* Hebrews 4:9—"There remaineth, therefore, a rest to the people of God."

*b)* Revelation 14:13—"Blessed are the dead who die in the Lord from henceforth. Yea, saith the Spirit, that they may rest from their labors."

No angel sat down, but Jesus sat down because His work was over.

B. The Destiny of Angels (v. 14)

"Are they not all ministering spirits, sent forth to minister for them who shall be heirs of salvation?"

The destiny of angels is to serve forever those who are the heirs of salvation—and that's us! What are they going to do for us?

1. Protecting the saints from danger

In 2 Kings 6, Elisha and his servant were being menaced by the King of Syria, and they didn't have any way to defend themselves. Verses 15-17 say, "When the servant of the man of God was risen early, and gone forth, behold, an host compassed the city, both with horses and chariots. And his servant said unto him, Alas, my master! What shall we do? And he answered, Fear not; for they who are with us are more than they who are with them. And Elisha prayed, and said, Lord, I pray thee, open his eyes, that he may see. And the Lord opened the eyes of the young man, and he saw; and, behold, the mountain was full of horses and chariots of fire round about Elisha." Those were angels. They protect the believer from temporal danger.

2. Delivering the saints from danger

It was angels who took Lot and his family out of Sodom. It was angels who stopped the lions' mouths when Daniel was thrown into a lions' den (Dan. 6:22).

It is marvelous to know that angels minister to us. And their destiny is to minister to us throughout eternity!

Jesus' destiny is to reign. Thus He is better than angels. We have discovered that the Son of God is superior to angels in every way through an examination of several Old Testament passages. Jesus is the Messiah. He is God in human flesh. He is the mediator of a New Covenant that is better than the Old. We have seen the deity of Jesus Christ established by His divine names: Son, Lord, and God. We have seen His deity established by His divine works: He created the universe and sustains it; He redeemed mankind and will eventually rule over all. His deity is established by divine attributes: He is omniscient, omnipotent, unchanging, and eternal. And His deity is established by the worship He deserves: He is the one to be worshiped by the angels and all creatures in the universe.

As a warning to those who would ignore what he wrote about the superiority of Christ, the writer of Hebrews says, "Therefore, we ought to give the more earnest heed to the things which we have heard, lest at any time we should let them slip. For if the word spoken by angels was steadfast, and every transgression and disobedience received a just recompense of reward, how shall we escape, if we neglect so great salvation?" (2:1-3). If God expected such a positive response to the law, which came through the angels, what response does He expect concerning the gospel, which came through Jesus Christ?

## Focusing on the Facts

1. What is the theme of the Bible? Support your answer with Scripture (see pp. 62-63).
2. Discuss the transition of Scripture (see pp. 63-64).
3. How can the veil be removed that lays over the hearts of the Jewish people in general (2 Cor. 3:14-16; see p. 64)?
4. How does the book of Hebrews describe the temporary nature of the Old Covenant (see pp. 65-66)?
5. What are some of the eternal things Hebrews discusses (see p. 66)?
6. What happened to the rituals of Judaism once the reality, Jesus Christ, came to man (see pp. 66-67)?
7. Who created the angels? What is the significance of that (Heb. 1:7; see p. 68)?
8. Why are the angels called "flames of fire" in Hebrews 1:7 (see pp. 68-69)?

9. What is the main difference between angels and Christ (Heb. 1:8; see p. 70)?
10. Name some verses that corroborate the deity of Christ (see pp. 70-71).
11. According to Hebrews 1:9, what motivated Jesus (see pp. 71-72)?
12. What will most Christians find out about themselves as they become more like Christ (see p. 72)?
13. When was Christ anointed (see p. 73)?
14. What can be inferred from the fact that Christ created the earth in the beginning (see p. 73)?
15. What does it mean that Christ is immutable (see p. 73)?
16. Describe what will happen to the earth during the Tribulation (Rev. 8:7-10, 12-13; see p. 74).
17. What is the ultimate destiny of Jesus Christ? When will that occur (see p. 75)?
18. How do angels serve God's people (see p. 76)?

## Pondering the Principles

1. The Hebrews had to learn that they no longer needed to hang onto their rituals because the reality came in the form of Jesus Christ. Perhaps you, although not in the same way as the Hebrews, are hanging on to rituals. They can be in the form of a ritualistic approach to going to church, serving on a certain committee or in a ministry, or even reading the Bible. Certainly we should do those things, but not as a matter of ritual. Are there some other things you are doing in a ritualistic manner? What do you need to do to change your ritualistic approach to one that is motivated by a love for Christ? Deepen your relationship with Christ by reading and studying His Word daily. In addition, ask God to show you how you might get to know Christ better.

2. Hebrews 1:9 says that Christ loves righteousness and hates iniquity. Name some actions in your life revealing that you love righteousness and hate iniquity. Are there actions in your life revealing that you hate righteousness because you love sin? What are they? One of the best treatments of righteousness versus unrighteousness is in 1 John. Spend the next half hour reading through 1 John. Record every verse reference dealing with righteousness and unrighteousness, noting the attitude and actions of those who adhere to each. Then determine how you might apply the most significant passages to further your active love of righteousness.

# 5

# The Tragedy of Neglecting Salvation

## Outline

Introduction
A. An Invitation
   1. The demand for a response
   2. The concern for a response
     *a*) By Paul
       (1) Romans 9:1-3
       (2) Romans 10:1
       (3) 1 Corinthians 9:19-23
     *b*) By Jesus
B. A Warning
   1. Those included
   2. Those excluded

Lesson
I. The Character of Christ (v. 1)
  A. Rejecting Without Cause
  B. Drifting Without Concern
    1. The basic definitions
     *a*) *Prosechō*
     *b*) *Pararheōmen*
    2. Their nautical significance
  C. Hearing Without Commitment
    1. The exhortation of Scripture
     *a*) Luke 9:44
     *b*) Proverbs 4:20-22
    2. The rejection of Scripture
    3. The bypassing of Scripture
II. The Certainty of Judgment (vv. 2-3*a*)
  A. The Free Choice
  B. The Fulfilled Condition
    1. The plan for angels
     *a*) Bringing forth a spoken law

## Introduction

Hell is undoubtedly full of people who did not actively oppose Jesus Christ but simply drifted into damnation by neglecting to respond to the gospel. Such people are in view in Hebrews 2:1-4. They are aware of the good news of salvation provided in Jesus Christ but aren't willing to commit their lives to Him. As a result, they drift past the call of God into eternal disaster. That is why these verses are urgent.

By way of reminder, Hebrews is an epistle addressed to three different groups of Jews residing in one particular community. One group was Jewish non-Christians who didn't believe anything about the gospel. A second group was Jewish Christians who were still hanging on to the rituals of Judaism. The third group was Jewish non-Christians who were intellectually convinced about the truths of the gospel but had never committed their lives to Christ. The writer of Hebrews had one purpose: to show all three groups that Jesus Christ brought a New Covenant that is better than the Old. He wanted to prove to the Jews that the Old Covenant was not wrong, but incomplete, for Jesus Christ is the fulfillment of the Old Covenant. To prove that the New Covenant is better, the writer of Hebrews discusses the important characters of the Old Covenant and shows Christ to be superior to all of them. In Hebrews 1:1-3 we see in general that Christ is better than everyone and everything. Then in verse 4-14 the writer deals specifically with Christ's superiority over angels.

A. An Invitation

In the midst of his treatise on angels, the writer of Hebrews gives an invitation to his readers so that they might apply what he has been saying about Christ. All along he's been saying that Christ is the greatest one, that He alone can purge sin, for He is God. He is the Creator, the exalted One, and is therefore worthy of our worship. But now he stops to give a personal invitation so that his readers and hearers might respond to what he's been saying. You might say that doctrine is punctuated by an invitation.

1. The demand for a response

The Word of God always demands a response—one must react to its message. And I add that any effective teacher must do more than just dispose of facts; he must warn, exhort, and extend an invitation.

2. The concern for a response

By the time the writer had written fourteen verses, he was impassioned. He truly cared about the salvation of his hearers. He was not so egocentric that he cared only for spewing out doctrine; he wanted a response. He not only exalted Christ but also cared that his hearers respond to Christ. A man may know a lot of truth and doctrine, but if he doesn't have a passionate concern for

81

how people react to it, he's not worth a nickel as a teacher.

*a)* By Paul

The apostle Paul was an excellent teacher. As great a theologian as he was with his masterful grasp of philosophy and logic, he was still an impassioned individual.

(1) Romans 9:1-3—After eight great chapters of treatise on the character of the gospel, Paul burst into a great display of emotion: "I say the truth in Christ, I lie not, my conscience also bearing me witness in the Holy Spirit, that I have great heaviness and continual sorrow in my heart. For I could wish that I myself were accursed from Christ for my brethren, my kinsmen according to the flesh." Paul had such a concern in his heart for his Jewish kinsmen to come to Christ that it ate away at him.

(2) Romans 10:1—"Brethren, my heart's desire and prayer to God for Israel is, that they might be saved." That reflects the character of a true teacher. Teaching does not include just academics but having a deep concern with how people respond.

(3) 1 Corinthians 9:19-23—"For though I am free from all men, yet have I made myself servant unto all, that I might gain the more. And unto the Jews I became as a Jew, that I might gain the Jews; to them that are under the law, as under the law, not being myself under the law, that I might gain them that are under the law. To them that are without law, as without law (being not without law to God, but under the law to Christ), that I might gain them that are without law. To the weak became I as weak, that I might gain the weak; I am made all things to all men, that I might by all means save some. And this I do for the gospel's sake."

*b)* By Jesus

In John 5:39-40 Jesus says, "Search the scriptures; for in them ye think ye have eternal life; and they are they which testify of me. And ye will not come to me, that ye might have life." Jesus also had a passionate concern that His hearers respond to His teaching.

In Hebrews 13:22 the book of Hebrews is referred to as a word of exhortation. It demands a response. And that's what the writer of Hebrews wants from the invitation that he interjects in the middle of his treatise on the superiority of Christ to angels. This invitation includes two things that all invitations must include—an exhortation and a warning.

B.  A Warning

The warning in Hebrews 2:1-4 is the first of five great warnings interjected throughout the book of Hebrews. Each one occurs in the middle of a treatise on the superiority of Christ. It's as if the writer can teach only so much before he has to confront his audience about their response. You can know all the truth there is to know about Jesus Christ and still go to hell if you never do anything about it.

1.  Those included

To whom is the warning directed? To Hebrew non-Christians who are intellectually convinced about the gospel but have never committed their life to Christ. You have probably met people like that who say, "I believe, but I'm not ready to make a commitment." They go to church and hear the Word of God. They know it's true, but they are not willing to commit themselves to Jesus Christ. They are like the man who believes a boat can hold him but never gets in.

2.  Those excluded

The warning could not be to Christians because they are never in danger of neglecting salvation since they already have it. They might neglect growth and discipleship, but they could never neglect salvation. The warning can't be directed to people who've never heard the gospel because they can't neglect what they don't know exists. The only group left is those non-Christians who are intellectually convinced of the gospel but not committed to it.

When the writer uses the words *we* and *us* in verses 1-3, is he including himself with those who were intellectually convinced? Is the author saying that he's not a Christian? No. The word *us* refers to the Jewish nationality that the author and the audience shared. We cannot build a theological case on the use of a pronoun. The author's willingness to identify himself with the readers does not mean that he is in the same spiritual condition they are. He seems to be saying, "All of us who have heard the gospel ought to accept it."

I believe the warning is directed to the intellectually convinced—those who have heard the gospel and know the facts about Jesus Christ but are not willing to receive Christ as Savior. That's the most tragic category of people in existence.

## Burning the Book

I will never forget a particular lady who came into my office and informed me that she was a prostitute. She said, "I need help; I'm desperate." So I presented the claims of Christ to her. Then I said, "Would you like to invite Jesus Christ into your life?" She said yes, and she prayed. I said, "Now, I want you to do something. Do you have your book with all your contacts?" She said she did. I said, "Let's light a match to it and burn it." She looked at me and said, "What do you mean?" I said, "If you want to live for Jesus Christ, and you've truly accepted His forgiveness and met Him as your Savior, then you need to prove it." She said to me, "That book is worth a lot of money. I don't want to burn it." She put it back in her purse and looked me right in the eye and said, "I guess I don't really want Jesus, do I?" Then she left.

When it came down to counting the cost, she wasn't ready. I don't know what the outcome of that poor woman has been. I do know she knew the facts and believed them, but she was not willing to make the sacrifice. What she kept wasn't worth anything compared to what she could have had in Jesus Christ.

The warning in Hebrews 2:1-4 is directed to those who know the truth but are hanging on the edge of a decision without making it. The writer wants to give them a big shove toward Jesus Christ. And this is not just directed toward a Jewish audience. It is also for any man who is on the edge of a decision for Christ but because of self-will, fear, sin, or impending persecution from family and friends, says no to Christ and continues to neglect Him. A man is a fool when he neglects to make the right decision. Why? There are three reasons: the character of Christ, the certainty of judgment, and the confirmation of God.

## Lesson

## I. THE CHARACTER OF CHRIST (v. 1)

"Therefore, we ought to give the more earnest heed to the things which we have heard, lest at any time we should let them slip."

What does that have to do with the character of Christ? "Therefore" is the key: It refers back to Jesus Christ. The writer is saying that because of who Christ is, you ought to pay attention to the things you have heard lest you slip away.

### A. Rejecting Without Cause

Based on Hebrews 1:1-14, Christ is the Son, the heir of all things, the one who made the world, the brightness of the glory of God, the exact image of His person, and the one who upholds all things by the word of His power. He purged our sins, is seated on the right hand of the majesty, is better than angels, and is chief of all. Even the angels worship Him and are His servants. He is forever and ever, anointed above all others, and the Lord of creation. What kind of a fool would reject Christ—the one who came into the world to die on a cross to forgive your sin, to pay the penalty you deserve, to show you love, to introduce you to God, and to give you blessing and joy beyond imagination? Christ's character makes rejection the most foolish act that a man could ever commit. Jesus was God in the world. To reject Jesus Christ is to reject God, which is to reject the reason for your existence. Because of the magnificence of the person of Christ, a man is a fool to reject the salvation He offers. I don't understand how people can know who Christ is and yet never commit their lives to Him. What a tragedy!

### B. Drifting Without Concern

There are two key Greek words in Hebrews 2:1: *prosechō*, which means "to give attention to" and *pararheōmen*, which means "to let slip."

1.  The basic definitions

    *a)   Prosechō*

    *Prosechō* is translated "to give the more earnest heed." The writer is saying that on the basis of who Christ is, we must give attention to the things we've heard about Him.

b) *Pararheōmen*

This word can be translated many ways. It can be used of something flowing or slipping past. It can be used of a ring slipping off a finger. It could even be used of something slipping into a wrong place. But it is most often used of something that has carelessly or thoughtlessly been allowed to slip away.

2. Their nautical significance

*Prosechō* means "to moor a ship"; *pararheōmen* can be used of a ship that has been carelessly allowed to drift past the harbor because the sailor forgot to attend to the steerage or chart the wind, tides, and current. Verse 1 could be translated this way: "Therefore, we must diligently anchor our lives to the things we have been taught lest the ship of life drift past the harbor of salvation and be lost forever." That is a graphic picture of what happens.

Men don't dive headlong into hell; they have more of a tendency to drift into it. Most people don't deliberately turn their backs on God; they almost imperceptibly slip past the harbor of salvation and are broken on the rocks of destruction. One writer, building on Shakespeare (*Julius Caesar* IV.iii.209), said,

> There is a tide in the affairs of men,
> Taken at its ebb, leads to victory
> Neglected, the shores and strands of time
> Are strewn with the wreckage.

This is not a picture of an ignorant or unbelieving sailor but of a careless one. So you had better take heed, unless slowly and imperceptibly you find yourself having slipped past the harbor of salvation and destroyed on the rocks.

C. Hearing Without Commitment

In Hebrews 2:1 the writer says that we need to take heed to the things we have heard. Many of the Jews had heard the gospel from apostolic missionaries but hadn't made a personal application.

1. The exhortation of Scripture

a) Luke 9:44—Jesus said, "Let these sayings sink down into your ears." It isn't enough to hear the words of Scripture; you need to let it get inside of you for it to make a change in your life.

*b)* Proverbs 4:20-22—Solomon said, "My son, attend to my words; incline thine ear unto my sayings. Let them not depart from thine eyes; keep them in the midst of thine heart. For they are life unto those that find them, and health to all their flesh." When you hear the Word of God, make it yours. The most dangerous thing you can do is to let it drift past your ears.

2. The rejection of Scripture

The Hebrew unbelievers had heard the Word, but they hadn't made a commitment. We know they had heard the voice of God because Hebrews 1:1-2 says, "God, who at sundry times and diverse manners spoke in time past unto the fathers by the prophets, hath in these last days spoken unto us by his Son." They had heard the voice of God in the Old Testament, in the person of Jesus Christ, and from apostolic missionaries, but they'd done nothing about it. A fool rejects the Word of God. The ultimate tragedy is for those people who continually hear the gospel to keep slipping carelessly, almost imperceptibly, to destruction.

3. The bypassing of Scripture

Hebrews 2:1 as translated in the King James Version seems to indicate that it is the Word of God that slips. But that's not true. The Greek text indicates that it is men who slip, not the Word. The Word of God never drifts; men drift from it. The harbor of salvation is Jesus Christ, and He never changes. Salvation is always available until the time a man slips past the harbor of grace. It makes me wonder how many thousands of people in hell were close to salvation. How many thousands were close to being safely moored and anchored, only to drift away forever through a failure to receive what they heard, and in many cases, actually believed to be true? Drifting is so quiet and easy, yet so damning. All you need to do to go to hell is do nothing. I don't understand how anyone who knows the character of Jesus Christ can reject Him. As a Christian who lives every day with Jesus Christ and experiences Him in my life, it is the greatest mystery to me that people wouldn't rush to Jesus and want everything He has for them.

### Drifting on an Ice Floe

English explorer William Edward Parry and his crew were explor-
ing the Arctic Ocean. At one point they endeavored to move
further north, so they charted their location by the stars and
began a difficult and treacherous march north. They walked hour
upon hour, and finally, totally exhausted, they stopped. They
took their bearings and discovered that they were farther south
than they were when they started! They then realized that they
had been walking on an ice floe that was traveling south faster
than they were walking north. I wonder how many people think
their good deed, their merits, and their religiousity is taking them
to God when in fact they're on an ice floe taking them away from
God faster than their own efforts are taking them any closer. They
will wake one day to find that they're in the midst of a disaster.

Don't be satisfied with religious feelings. Don't be satisfied with
going to church. Don't be satisfied with being married to a
Christian spouse. Don't be satisfied with church activity. You are
drifting into hell if you haven't made a personal commitment to
Him. A man is a fool to reject salvation.

II. THE CERTAINTY OF JUDGMENT (vv. 2-3a)

"For if the word spoken by angels [the Old Covenant] was
steadfast, and every transgression and disobedience received a
just recompense of reward, how shall we escape, if we neglect so
great salvation."

If no one got away with breaking the covenant brought by angels,
no one will get away with breaking the covenant brought by our
Lord.

A. The Free Choice

The Holy Spirit is arguing from the lesser to the greater with
the two testaments in mind. The one testament was the
revelation of the law that came by angels. Any breach of that
law, or any disobedience to it, was followed by severe and
just punishment. The other revelation came through Christ.
Since it came through a greater mediator, the Son of God, it
is a greater covenant and consequently brings about equal or
greater punishment. A man is a fool to think he can escape
from the punishment of the new and greater covenant if no
man ever escaped the punishment of the old. There are
people who believe that God is a God of love and grace, yet
not of justice. If you do not receive Jesus Christ, God's justice
can only condemn you. The choice is yours.

88

Verse 2 says, "Every transgression and disobedience received a just recompense of reward." The word *every* indicates there was no escape from the law of the Old Covenant. Likewise, there is no escape from the law of the New Covenant. You don't have to keep a bunch of laws in the New Covenant; you only have to keep one—to believe in Jesus Christ and receive Him as your Lord. That is what secures to you the New Covenant and freedom from punishment. In Romans 8:1 Paul says, "There is, therefore, now no condemnation to them who are in Christ Jesus." There is no judgment for anyone who is in Christ. There's only one law in the New Covenant—the necessity of receiving Jesus Christ by faith. If a man couldn't neglect the revelation that came through angels, how could he neglect the revelation that came through the Lord Himself?

B. The Fulfilled Condition

Hebrews 2:2 says, "For if the word spoken by angels was steadfast." The word *if* represents what is known in Greek as a fulfilled condition. In other words, it doesn't mean "maybe"; it means "absolutely." The verse could be translated, "Since the word spoken by angels was steadfast."

1. The plan for angels

   a) Bringing forth a spoken law

      Notice that verse 2 says, "The word spoken by angels." Why are the Old Testament commandments connected with the angels? Because the angels were instrumental in bringing the Ten Commandments to Israel.

      (1) Psalm 68:17—"The chariots of God are twenty thousand, even thousands of angels; the Lord is among them, as in Sinai, in the holy place." Where did Moses get the law? On Mount Sinai. Angels were also at Sinai.

      (2) Deuteronomy 33:2—Moses said, "The Lord came from Sinai, and rose up from Seir unto them; he shined forth from Mount Paran, and he came with ten thousands of saints [angels]. From his right hand went a fiery law for them." That indicates angels were involved in the bringing of the law.

(3) Acts 7:38—In referring to Moses, Stephen said, "This is he that was in the church in the wilderness with the angel who spoke to him in Mount Sinai." When Moses was in Sinai, an angel spoke to him. Verse 53 says he "received the law by the disposition of angels."

Angels were at Sinai. They were instrumental in the bringing of the law.

b) Bringing forth a steadfast law

The law the angels spoke, primarily the Ten Commandments, was steadfast. That means if the law was broken, the law broke the lawbreaker. There wasn't any out. If a person committed adultery, he was stoned. If a person worshiped false gods and blasphemed God, he was stoned. The law was inviolable; punishment for breaking it was certain.

2. The punishment for sin

Verse 2 says, "Every transgression and disobedience received a just recompense of reward." That means the law punished every sin.

a) The definition of sin

There are two kinds of sin:

(1) "Transgression"

The Greek word *parabasis* means "to step across a line." That's a willful act of sin—an overt sin of commission, a purposeful sin.

(2) "Disobedience"

The Greek word for disobedience here (*parakoē*) refers to imperfect hearing. This kind of sin is a deliberate shutting of the ears to the commands, warnings, and invitations of God. It is a sin of neglect or omission. It is a sin of doing nothing when you should be doing something.

There are only two kinds of sin, and they involve what you do and what you don't do. Every sin was covered by the law. Both types of sin were breaches of Old Testament law and they received a just punishment.

*b)* The details of punishment

(1) Its severity

The punishments in Old Testament days were severe.

(*a*) Leviticus 24:14-16—"Bring forth him who hath cursed outside the camp; and let all that heard him lay their hands upon his head, and let all the congregation stone him. And thou shalt speak unto the children of Israel, saying, Whosoever curseth his God shall bear his sin. And he who blasphemeth the name of the Lord, he shall surely be put to death, and all the congregation shall certainly stone him; as well the sojourner as he who is born in the land, when he blasphemeth the name of the Lord, shall be put to death." Now that's a severe law. God wanted to make sure Israel's purity was maintained by dealing immediately with all false prophets and blasphemers.

(*b*) Numbers 15:30-36—"The soul that doeth anything presumptuously, whether he is born in the land, or a sojourner, the same reproacheth the Lord; and that soul shall be cut off from among his people. Because he hath despised the word of the Lord, and hath broken his commandment, that soul shall be utterly cut off; his iniquity shall be upon him. And while the children of Israel were in the wilderness, they found a man who gathered sticks upon the sabbath day. And they who found him gathering sticks brought him unto Moses and Aaron, and unto all the congregation. And they put him in prison, because it was not declared what should be done to him. And the Lord said unto Moses, The man shall be surely put to death; all the congregation shall stone him with stones outside the camp. And all the congregation brought him outside the camp, and stoned him with stones, and he died; as the Lord commanded Moses." Picking up sticks on the sabbath may seem to be a trivial thing to warrant a stoning, but the principle is the issue: He was

91

defying the law of God, and the punishment for breaking the law was inviolable.

(c) Numbers 25:1-9—"Israel abode in Shittim, and the people began to commit harlotry with the daughters of Moab. And they called the people unto the sacrifices of their gods; and the people did eat, and bowed down to their gods. And Israel joined himself unto Baal-peor; and the anger of the Lord was kindled against Israel. And the Lord said unto Moses, Take all the heads of the people, and hang them up before the Lord against the sun, that the fierce anger of the Lord may be turned away from Israel. And Moses said unto the judges of Israel, Slay ye every one his men that were joined unto Baal-peor. And, behold, one of the children of Israel came and brought unto his brethren a Midianitish woman in the sight of Moses and in the sight of all the congregation of the children of Israel who were weeping before the door of the tabernacle of the congregation. And when Phinehas, the son of Eleazar, the son of Aaron the priest, saw it, he rose up from among the congregation, and took a javelin in his hand; and he went after the man of Israel into the tent, and thrust both of them through, the man of Israel, and the woman through her abdomen. So the plague was stayed from the children of Israel. And those that died in the plague were twenty and four thousand." God had to do that to maintain purity in Israel. He defended them and kept them from false gods. The ones who were slain were not of God but of Satan. And God dealt strictly with them.

(d) Deuteronomy 17:2-7—"If there be found among you, within any of thy gates which the Lord thy God giveth thee, man or woman who hath wrought wickedness in the sight of the Lord thy God, in transgressing his covenant, and hath gone and served other gods, and worshiped them, either the sun, or moon, or any of the host of heaven, which I have not commanded, and it be told thee, and thou hast heard of it, and inquired diligently, and, behold, it is true, and the thing certain, that such abomination is wrought in Israel; then shalt thou bring forth that man or that woman, who hath committed that wicked thing, unto thy gates, even that man or that woman, and shalt stone them with stones, till they die. At the mouth of two witnesses, or three witnesses, shall he that is worthy of death be put to death; but at the mouth of one witness he shall not be put to death. The hands of the witnesses shall be first upon him to put him to death, and afterward the hands of all the people. So thou shalt put the evil away from among you." Why did God do all that? Verse 13 says so that "all the people shall hear, and fear, and do no more presumptuously." If the consequence is made strict enough, the people will obey.

(e) Deuteronomy 27:26—"Cursed be he who confirmeth not all the words of this law to do them. And all the people shall say, Amen."

(f) Jude 5—"I will, therefore, put you in remembrance, though ye once knew this, that the Lord, having saved the people out of the land of Egypt, afterward destroyed them that believed not."

If unbelief was severely punished under the Old Covenant, you can be sure it will be even more severe under the New Covenant. That's the point of Hebrews 2:2-3: "If the word spoken by angels was steadfast, and every transgression and disobedience received a just recompense of reward, how shall we escape, if we neglect so great salvation?"

(2) Its justice

People like to accuse God of not being just. But according to verse 2, God *is* just. He has never done anything unjust in His existence. Every punishment was a deterrent to the sin that He

93

wanted to stop. He punished only those who had determined to defy Him. So He removed them for the sake of those who were pure and holy and wanted to live for Him.

(*a*) The principle

God's judgment on Israel was severe because they knew better. And that leads us to an important principle: punishment is always related to light. The more light you have, the more severe your punishment will be.

i) Matthew 11:20-24—"Then began he [Jesus] to upbraid the cities in which most of his mighty works were done, because they repented not. Woe unto thee, Chorazin! Woe unto thee, Bethsaida! For if the mighty works, which were done in you, had been done in Tyre and Sidon, they would have repented long ago in sackcloth and ashes. But I say unto you, It shall be more tolerable for Tyre and Sidon at the day of judgment, than for you. And thou, Capernaum, which art exalted unto heaven, shalt be brought down to hades; for if the mighty works, which have been done in thee, had been done in Sodom, it would have remained until this day. But I say unto you, That it shall be more tolerable for the land of Sodom in the day of judgment, than for thee." The more you know, the greater the punishment. Sodom and Gomorrah, and Tyre and Sidon were punished, but in no way like Capernaum, Bethsaida, and Chorazin will be punished. They had known not only the truths of the Old Testament but the revelation of God's Messiah as well.

ii) Mark 12:38-40—Jesus said, "Beware of the scribes, who love to go in long clothing, and love salutations in the market places, and the chief seats in the synagogues, and the uppermost places at feasts; who devour widows' houses, and for a pretense make long prayers; these shall receive greater condemnation." Did you know that there are degrees of punishment in hell? And the worst of hell belongs to those who rejected the most light.

iii) Luke 12:47-48—Jesus said, "And that servant, who knew his lord's will, and prepared not himself, neither did according to his will, shall be beaten with many stripes. But he that knew not, and did commit things worthy of stripes, shall be beaten with few stripes. For unto whomsoever much is given, of him shall be much required."

Since the law brought by angels had stern and severe judgment, how much more severe will judgment be on those who not only have the old law but also the New Covenant in Christ, yet still willfully reject it! That truth is pointed out clearly and explicitly in Hebrews 10:28-29: "He that despised Moses' law died without mercy under two or three witnesses; of how much sorer punishment, suppose ye, shall he be thought worthy, who hath trodden under foot the Son of God, and hath counted the blood of the covenant, with which he was sanctified, an unholy thing, and hath done despite unto the Spirit of grace?" If you think punishment was bad under Moses' law, it will be that much worse for one who knows the truth of Jesus Christ, makes a mental assent to it, and then treads the blood of Jesus Christ under his feet.

(b) The pit

The man who knows the gospel, who has intellectually understood it and believed it, yet drifts away, will experience the severest punishment of all. Many people in hell are experiencing it now, for hell is a real place. The New Testament calls it a place of everlasting fire (Matt. 25:41) where the worm does not die and the fire is not quenched (Mark 9:43-44). It's called a lake of fire that burns with brimstone (Rev. 19:20). It's called a bottomless pit (Rev. 9:11). It is called black darkness (Jude 13). And it's called outer darkness, where there is continual weeping and gnashing of teeth (Matt. 22:13).

How can a man escape judgment if he rejects the New Covenant of Christ? He can't. There is no way to escape if we neglect such a great salvation. Romans 2:3 says, "And thinkest thou this, O man, that judgest them who do such things, and doest the same, that thou shalt escape the judgment of God?"

III. THE CONFIRMATION OF GOD (vv. 3-4)

A. Confirmed by the Preacher of the Gospel (v. 3a)

"How shall we escape, if we neglect so great salvation, which at the first began to be spoken by the Lord."

The word for "Lord" in the Septuagint is the translation of the word *Jehovah*. This is another indication that Jesus is God. He is the Jehovah God of the Old Testament. Verse 3 says that the gospel was first spoken by the Lord. Christ was the first preacher of the gospel of repentance. Luke 4:16-21 says, "He came to Nazareth, where he had been brought up; and, as his custom was, he went into the synagogue on the sabbath day, and stood up to read. And there was delivered unto him the book of the prophet, Isaiah. And when he had opened the book, he found the place where it was written, The Spirit of the Lord is upon me, because he hath anointed me to preach the gospel to the poor; he hath sent me to heal the brokenhearted, to preach deliverance to the captives, and recovering of sight to the blind, to set at liberty them that are bruised, to preach the acceptable year of the Lord. And he closed the book, and he gave it again to the minister, and sat down. . . . And he began to say unto them, This day is this scripture fulfilled in your ears." The people became upset because He was claiming to be the Messiah. Jesus was the first preacher of the gospel.

B. Confirmed by the Hearers of the Gospel (v. 3b)

"And was confirmed unto us by them that heard him."

The believing Jews who were the object of this letter didn't hear the gospel from Christ Himself; they heard it from apostolic missionaries. The Lord preached it first, but it was passed on by those who heard Him. These Jews were the second generation of those who heard the message.

C. Confirmed by the Works of the Gospel (v. 4)

"God also bearing them witness, both with signs and wonders, and with diverse miracles and gifts of the Holy Spirit, according to his own will."

1. The people

   a) Christ

   When Jesus preached the gospel, He did miracles that made what He said believable. He said, "Though ye believe not me, believe the works" (John 10:38). Jesus claimed to be from God, and then made it obvious that He was really from God. Nicodemus came to Him by night and said, "No man can do these miracles that thou doest, except God be with him" (John 3:2). Jesus confirmed His ministry by His own miracles. And Peter confirms that on the day of Pentecost in Acts 2:22: "Ye men of Israel, hear these words: Jesus of Nazareth, a man approved of God among you by miracles and wonders and signs."

   b) Apostles and prophets

   The same things Peter talked about on the day of Pentecost were the same confirming signs given to the second generation preachers—the apostles. Many of their listeners no doubt said, "Why should we believe them? There have always been many false teachers around. How can we know they're for real?" So God gave His messengers the ability to do the same things Jesus had done— signs, wonders, and miracles. Jesus Himself told His own disciples, "Greater works than these shall [ye] do, because I go unto my Father" (John 14:12). The apostles performed astounding miracles, such as raising the dead and healing people.

   If men were to argue that the gospel of Jesus Christ couldn't possibly come from the mouths of the apostles, then they were arguing in spite of the confirmation from God. What the apostles said was not their own opinion; it was divine truth substantiated by signs, wonders, and miracles. Read chapters five through nineteen of Acts and you will see the many miracles that attended the ministry of these men.

God was saying, "Believe them. They're from Me, and it's proven by their ability to do miracles."

2.  The works

The words "signs, wonders, and miracles" are synonyms. They each refer to all the supernatural things the apostles did. Yet they confirmed the Word not only with such things but also with gifts of the Holy Spirit.

*a)* Their source

Hebrews 2:4 says that the gifts of the Spirit were done "according to his own will." That phrase seems to be put there to keep people from being confused about the source of certain gifts. In a conversation I had with Dr. Earl Radmacher, the president of Western Conservative Baptist Seminary, he told me he received a pamphlet in the mail that gave steps for obtaining the Holy Spirit. Supposedly, if you said "Praise the Lord" and "Hallelujah" three times faster than normal for a period of ten minutes, you would lapse into a strange language and receive the Holy Spirit. That's about as ridiculous as anything you'll ever hear. But the apostles performed signs, wonders, miracles, and gifts of the Holy Spirit given to them by the will of God.

*b)* Their significance

There are many gifts of the Holy Spirit—Romans 12, 1 Corinthians 12, and Ephesians 4 list the gifts. But the gifts referred to in Hebrews 2:4 were miraculous gifts for the sake of confirmation.

(1) Their supernatural power

(*a*) 2 Corinthians 12:12—Paul said, "Truly the signs of an apostle were wrought among you in all patience, in signs, and wonders, and mighty deeds."

(*b*) Romans 15:19—Paul said, "Through mighty signs and wonders, by the power of the Spirit of God, so that from Jerusalem, and round about unto Illyricum, I have fully preached the gospel of Christ." Paul was an apostle and he had the ability to do miracles.

(c) Acts 14:3—Luke said, "A long time, therefore, abode they [Paul and Barnabas] speaking boldly in the Lord, who gave testimony unto the word of his grace, and granted signs and wonders to be done by their hands."

(d) Acts 15:32—Luke said, "And Judas and Silas, being prophets also themselves, exhorted the brethren with many words, and confirmed them." How did they confirm their words? With signs, miracles, and gifts of the Holy Spirit.

(2) Their special purpose

(a) The confirmation

What were the gifts of the Spirit? I believe there were four: healing, miracles, tongues (languages), and interpretation of tongues. They were the four special confirming gifts used to prove to people, by supernatural acts, that the apostles and prophets spoke from God.

(b) The cessation

I also believe that those gifts all ceased with the apostolic era. There is no need for them to exist today because there is no need to confirm the Word. If someone says, "Thus saith the Lord," all you need to do is match up what he says with God's Word. Benjamin Warfield, the great Bible scholar, said, "These miraculous gifts were part of the credentials of the apostles as the authoritative agents of God in founding the church. Their function thus confined them distinctively in the apostolic church, and they necessarily passed away with it."

First Corinthians 14:22 says, "Tongues are for a sign, not to them that believe, but to them that believe not." Those gifts never had any importance for believers; they served as confirmation to unbelievers that the apostles and prophets spoke for God. When the Word was established, such miracles ceased.

There are three reasons that a man is a fool to neglect salvation: the character of Christ, the certainty of judgment, and the confirmation of God. God has attested to the gospel with signs, wonders, miracles, gifts, and now in the miracle of His written Word. Let it not be said of you that you neglected Jesus Christ. History tells us that hours of neglect cost Napoleon Waterloo. And neglecting Christ's salvation will cost you eternal blessing and joy and bring you damnation. Don't be so foolish that you drift past God's grace.

### Focusing on the Facts

1. What does the writer of Hebrews do in the midst of his discussion of angels? Why (see p. 81)?
2. What must any effective teacher do (see p. 81)?
3. Whom did the writer of Hebrews have in mind when he gave the warning in Hebrews 2:1-4 (see p. 83)?
4. Who is a person rejecting when he rejects Jesus Christ (see p. 85)?
5. What are the two key Greek words in Hebrews 2:1? Define them both, and explain their significance (see pp. 85-86).
6. Ultimately, how do most men wind up in hell? Do they deliberately choose to go there, or do they drift into it? Explain (see pp. 86-87).
7. What is the one law in the New Testament (see p. 89)?
8. Explain how the angels were instrumental in bringing the Old Testament to Israel (see pp. 89-90).
9. What are the two kinds of sin? Define each one (see p. 90).
10. Describe the severity of punishments in Old Testament days (see pp. 91-93).
11. What principle can be gleaned from God's severe punishment of Israel? Give some verses that show this principle in action (see pp. 94-95).
12. What are some of the biblical names for hell (see pp. 95-96)?
13. Who was the first preacher of the gospel? (see p. 96)?
14. How did God confirm the preaching of the apostles and prophets (Heb. 2:4; see pp. 96-97)?
15. What do the words "signs, wonders, and miracles" in Hebrews 2:4 refer to (see p. 98)?
16. What were the gifts of the Spirit referred to in Hebrews 2:4? What was their special purpose (see pp. 98-99)?

### Pondering the Principles

1. When you present the gospel to an unbeliever, or teach or share God's Word to a believer, is your primary concern to generate a response from your listener? If it isn't, it should be. Look up the

following verses regarding the apostle Paul's commitment to share the gospel with others: Romans 9:1-3; 10:1; 1 Corinthians 2:1-4; 9:19-23; 10:33. Perhaps you could apply something you have learned from Paul's example. Make the commitment to do so.

2. First Corinthians 11:28 says that a person should examine himself before he participates in communion. Examining ourselves is something we should practice more than we do. Take a few minutes to examine yourself in terms of your own salvation. Are you trying to live the Christian life in your own power—working hard to get closer to God while you are actually slipping past the harbor of salvation? Make sure that you have made a true commitment to Jesus Christ as Lord in your life. If you're sure you have, yet you feel as if you are being frustrated in your efforts to live the Christian life, ask God to give you insight. Approach your pastor or a Christian friend to help you solidify your faith in Christ.

3. Review the two definitions of sin on page 90. Write those definitions somewhere in your Bible. Look carefully at those definitions and ask God to reveal the sins in your life that correspond to each definition. Learn to easily identify those sins that fall in the area of neglect or omission. It is usually easy for us to remember when we have defied God, but it is not so easy for us to be sensitive to times when we have failed to do something we should have.

# 6
# The Recovery of Man's Lost Destiny

## Outline

Introduction
A. The Purpose of Hebrews
B. The Promise of God
   1. Fulfilled in prophecy
   2. Fulfilled in types
      *a)* The sacrifices
      *b)* The tabernacles
      *c)* The Passover lambs

Review

Lesson
I. Man's Destiny Revealed by God (vv. 5-8*a*)
  A. The Role of Angels (v. 5)
    1. In the future world
    2. In the present world
      *a)* Satan
      *b)* Holy angels
        (1) Daniel 10:20
        (2) Daniel 12:1
  B. The Role of Man (vv. 6-8*a*)
    1. Created to be king
    2. Made lower than the angels
      *a)* The designation of time
      *b)* The difference between men and angels
      *c)* The design for the future
        (1) The possession of the kingdom
          (*a*) Daniel 7:18
          (*b*) Daniel 7:27
        (2) The preview of the kingdom
          (*a*) The equality between men and angels

## Introduction

A. The Purpose of Hebrews

The book of Hebrews is dedicated to the majesty and the absolute superiority of Jesus Christ over anyone and anything, particularly over everything related to Judaism prior to the coming of Christ. It is incongruous to accept the Old Covenant and reject Jesus Christ, who is the fulfillment of the Old Covenant. The Holy Spirit presents Christ as God—the center of the universe and all worship. All things converge on Christ and all things radiate from Him. He is the key to every page and every chapter in Hebrews. He is seen as the holiest among the mighty and the mightiest among the holy. He is seen as the King of kings and Lord of lords. One day He will come and put all enemies under His feet, and He will reign supreme. The entire universe exists by and for Jesus Christ, and it hastens to His coronation—the day when the world for which He shed His blood will belong to Him.

The message of Hebrews from beginning to end is the superiority of Jesus Christ. When Christ came as the Messiah of Israel, the One who fulfilled all the Old Testament promises, the Jewish nation rejected Him. They made the mistake of favoring the pictures, types, symbols, and rituals of the Old Testament over the reality. So the writer of Hebrews attempts to show them their folly.

B.  The Promise of God

Throughout Hebrews, the Holy Spirit uses Old Testament passages to prove the superiority of Jesus Christ. The Jewish people needed to understand that Christ is the redeemer God had promised. He is the redeemer all true saints hoped for. And He is the only redeemer men will ever know. How were people saved in the Old Testament? They weren't saved by keeping the law; they were saved by believing the promise of God. How is someone saved in the New Testament? By believing the promise of God. It's the same promise, only from a different perspective.

Redemptive history in the Old Testament focuses on Christ. The Old Testament was like a kindergarten in that God's people were trained in divine pictures but were told to look for better things to come. And those better things finally came in Jesus Christ. In the Old Testament, God taught His children the alphabet. In the New Testament, He taught them to put the letters together, and they spelled Christ. It is Christ who fulfills all the pictures of the Old Testament.

1.  Fulfilled in prophecy

Isaiah 53 is a prophecy of the Messiah's death, and it is fulfilled to the absolute letter in Christ's death. Psalm 22 describes the crucifixion of Christ. It even tells us what He would say on the cross. Isaiah 7:14 prophesies that the Christ would be born of a virgin. Micah 5:2 predicts that He would be born in Bethlehem. Every Messianic prophecy in the Old Testament resolves itself in Jesus Christ. That's why Jesus said, "Think not that I am come to destroy the law, or the prophets; I am not come to destroy, but to fulfill" (Matt. 5:17).

2.  Fulfilled in types

Types are Old Testament pictures of Christ—either of His person or His work. The type could be a man, an event, an animal, a situation—anything that pictures Christ.

*a)* The sacrifices

When a sacrifice was made, its blood was sprinkled on the Ark of the Covenant (the symbol of the presence of God), thus appeasing God's anger over sin. The sprinkling of blood pictured a more noble and perfect blood that would be shed once for all at some future time (Heb. 10:14). Jesus shed His perfect blood and became the antitype, or the fulfillment of that type.

*b)* The tabernacles

When the children of Israel wandered in the wilderness, they dwelled in tents, or tabernacles. That was a type of one great Person whose residence in human flesh was but a temporary humble dwelling that was beneath His dignity. Jesus said He had come to tabernacle or dwell among men (Heb. 8:2).

*c)* The Passover lambs

The Passover lambs allude to another Lamb who would shed His blood and bring eternal deliverance (1 Cor. 5:7).

There are so many types of the death of Christ in the Old Testament that the apostle Paul was prompted to say, "Christ died for our sins according to the scriptures" (1 Cor. 15:3). When Paul said that, the New Testament had not been completed, so what scripture was he referring to? The Old Testament. Christ died for our sins according to the Old Testament. Throughout the Old Testament are numerous pictures of Jesus' death for us, both in prophecy and type.

To accept the Old Covenant and reject Christ is ridiculous because it is a rejection of everything the Old Testament pointed to, and that was the Jewish dilemma. Jesus told the Jewish leaders, "Search the scriptures; for in them ye think ye have eternal life; and they are they which testify of me" (John 5:39). What was He referring to? The Old Testament. Later on the road to Emmaus He said, "O foolish ones, and slow of heart to believe all that the prophets have spoken! . . . And beginning at Moses and all the prophets, he expounded unto them, in all the scriptures, the things concerning himself" (Luke 24:25, 27). To reject Jesus Christ is absurd if you accept the Old Testament. In the book of Hebrews the Holy Spirit attempts to show the Jewish people that Jesus is the fulfillment of the Old Covenant and that He must be received as such or everything is meaningless.

## Review

First the author of Hebrews, by the inspiration of the Holy Spirit, had to show that Jesus is superior to angels because the Old Covenant was brought by angels. He does so by showing that Jesus is the fulfillment of all God did in the Old Testament. That presentation warranted an invitation from the writer in Hebrews 2:1-4. Since Jesus is God, and since He is superior to angels, there ought to be a response to Him.

## Lesson

Beginning in Hebrews 2:5, the writer returns to a discussion of the superiority of Christ over angels. He presents a fantastic point in verse 5 (and then elucidates it in verses 6-9): "For unto the angels hath he not put in subjection the world to come, of which we speak." What is he saying? That God will not give angels subjection of the world to come. Jesus Christ is the sovereign of the world to come, which means He is superior to angels.

Hebrews 2:5-9 accomplishes several things. First, it is another tremendous proof that Jesus is better than angels. Second, it answers a potential objection: Since Jesus was a man, how could He be superior to angels? And third, these verses reveal the only hope for man's recovery of his lost destiny. Man today has lost the meaning of his existence. This passage is going to teach us what man's destiny is and how he can recover it. We'll look at three simple points: man's destiny revealed by God, man's destiny restricted by sin, and man's destiny recovered by Christ.

I. MAN'S DESTINY REVEALED BY GOD (vv. 5-8a)

A.  The Role of Angels (v. 5)

"For unto the angels hath he not put in subjection the world to come, of which we speak."

God never promised to subject the coming world to angels. In fact, Hebrews 1:14 says that angels are "sent forth to minister for them who shall be heirs of salvation." In the world to come, angels will be ministers, not rulers.

The phrase "put in subjection" is the translation of the Greek word *hupotassō*, which is a military term used for arranging soldiers in order under a commanding general. It refers to a system of administration. God ordains every power (Rom. 13:1). He gives out the right to rule, and He chooses the various sovereigns. Angels will not be among them in the world to come. Certainly the world to come is the world of perfection. It will be a great and glorious world. Whoever reigns in it must be glorious beyond glory, but it won't be angels.

1. In the future world

Who is going to rule in the age to come? Men. Thus, the authority of angels over men at present is only temporary. An important point to understand is that the Greek word translated "world" in verse 5 is not *kosmos*, which means "the system" or *aion*, which means "the ages"; it is *oikoumenē*. The Greek word *oikos* means "house" and *oikoumenē* means "inhabitants." The writer is referring to the inhabited earth. Amillennialists maintain that there is no future earthly kingdom. But this verse clearly indicates that an inhabited earth is to come. That earth is not our present one. It will be replaced by the great millennial kingdom. All the creatures that go into that new earth will be totally different. The animals will be different. Even the people will all be redeemed. Someone will have the sovereignty in that inhabited earth, but it won't belong to angels.

2. In the present world

The world to come will not be put in subjection of angels. But the world to go, which is this one, is right now in subjection to angels.

a) Satan

Who is the number one fallen angel? Satan. Who is the prince of this world? Satan. Who is the sovereign of this world? Satan. Ephesians 6 tells us this world is ruled by demons, that they are sovereigns in the world. They're referred to as principalities, powers, rulers of the darkness of this world, and spiritual wickedness in high offices (Eph. 6:12). Those are ranks of demons that are ruling the world.

b) Holy angels

Satan and his fallen angels are not the only ones who rule in this world; even the holy angels now have a kind of sovereignty.

(1) Daniel 10:20—An angel told Daniel, "Knowest thou why I come unto thee? And now will I return to fight with the prince of Persia; and when I am gone forth, lo, the prince of Greece shall come." The rule of this earth is now in the hands of both fallen and holy angels, and this "joint" rulership obviously involves extreme conflict.

(2) Daniel 12:1—"And at that time shall Michael stand up, the great prince who standeth for the children of thy people." Michael is seen as a defender of God's people.

Technically our present earth is subject to angels. But the earth to come won't be. The only reason our present earth is subject to angels is that men lost the sovereignty God gave them in the beginning. But in the kingdom, that sovereignty will be restored to men. That is important to understand because this argument is sure to come: Since Jesus was a man, how can He be better than angels? That's no argument at all because when God made the earth, He intended for it to be subject to men, not angels. But Satan stole it from men. The inhabited earth is under the sovereignty of angels, both holy and unholy, battling over it. Yet it is God's final intention for man to have his sovereignty restored.

B. The Role of Man (vv. 6-8*a*)

"But one in a certain place testified, saying, What is man, that thou art mindful of him? Or the son of man, that thou visitest him? Thou madest him a little lower than the angels; thou crownedst him with glory and honor, and didst set him over the works of thy hands; thou hast put all things in subjection under his feet. For in that he put all in subjection under him, he left nothing that is not put under him."

The earth to come will be under the control of men. And that's revealed in verses 6-8, which are direct quotes from Psalm 8, which describe God's destiny for man. They refer to man, not to the Messiah.

**Emphasizing the Divine Instrument**

The writer does a clever thing in Hebrews 2:6 by stating, "But one in a certain place testified." He is referring to David's testimony in Psalm 8. The writer was not ignorant of Scripture; he knew

David wrote Psalm 8. Yet throughout the book of Hebrews he didn't name any Old Testament author, perhaps because he wanted to diminish the human instrument and emphasize the voice of God. He was so concerned that his Hebrew readers understand who really wrote the Old Testament that he never ascribed it to anyone but God. That's why he passed over David.

God's original destiny for man was to be king of the earth and for everything in existence to be in subjection to him. David was asking, "Why? What is man that You would do this for him?" In comparison to the universe, man seems to be an insignificant dot in the middle of infinity. What right do we have to be so much in the mind of God? Yet David said, "Thou madest him a little lower than the angels; thou crownedst him with glory and honor, and didst set him over the works of thy hands; thou hast put all things in subjection under his feet" (Heb. 2:7-8).

1.   Created to be king

Man is king. God made him that way. And that is man's destiny as revealed by God. He made a race of kings. David undoubtedly took his thoughts from Genesis 1:26-31: "God said, Let us make man in our image, after our likeness; and let them have dominion over the fish of the sea, and over the fowl of the air, and over the cattle, and over all the earth, and over every creeping thing that creepeth upon the earth. . . . And God blessed them, and God said unto them, Be fruitful, and multiply, and fill the earth, and subdue it; and have dominion over the fish of the sea, and over the fowl of the air, and over every living thing that moveth upon the earth. And God said, Behold, I have given you every herb bearing seed, which is upon the face of all the earth, and every tree, in which is the fruit of a tree yielding seed; to you it shall be for food. And to every beast of the earth, and to every fowl of the air, and to every thing that creepeth upon the earth, wherein there is life, I have given every green herb for food: and it was so. And God saw every thing that he had made, and, behold, it was very good." God's original design for man in his innocence was to be king over the undefiled earth. Hebrews 2:7 tells us that God also created man a little lower than the angels. So the chain of command is God, angels, man, and earth.

Hebrews 2:6 includes the phrase "son of man." Some interpret that to be a reference to Christ, but I believe it is a reference to men. Son of man is simply a Hebrew way of referring to mankind. For example, Ezekiel is frequently called the son of man—he was born of man. So David was asking, "What is so good about man that You've made him king of the earth? Why have You visited him?" The word translated "visitest" in the Greek text refers to God's desire to benefit man. Why does God hold such importance for frail humanity? Man must be of great importance for God to make him king.

2. Made lower than the angels

Notice that Hebrews 2:7 says, "Thou madest him a little lower than the angels." That does not mean he was made lower spiritually, or that God loved man less than angels. Man was made lower in the sense that he is physical and angels are spiritual. Angels are heavenly, and man is earthly.

*a)* The designation of time

The phrase translated "a little lower" in Hebrews 2:7 is a designation of time in the Greek language. Verse 7 should be translated, "Thou madest him for a little time lower than the angels." From the beginning of creation God knew that the ultimate destiny of man would not be something lower than angels. He set up only a temporary chain of command. God has a destiny for man that sets him up as king on an equal footing with angels. It is only for a little time at the beginning that God has made man lower than angels.

*b)* The difference between men and angels

In what way was man made a little lower than the angels? At the time of his creation, man was confined by a physical body while angels were able to move freely as spirits. Man was confined to the earth—he could not ascend into the supernatural. Angels were not confined to the supernatural—they could move about on the earth whenever they wanted. Man's only communion with God was when God revealed Himself to man. Angels have access to the throne of God whenever they desire. Angels are supernatural; man, even when sinless, was still natural. Angels are spirit beings; man was made out of the dust of the earth. After Satan's rebellion, the faithful angels were secured in holiness forever; after Adam rebelled, all men were cursed with him. In Adam, all died (1 Cor. 15:22). The key is this: There was no possibility for angels to die, yet there was with men. God said, "Of the tree of the knowledge of good and evil, thou shalt not eat of it; for in the day that thou eatest thereof thou shalt surely die" (Gen. 2:17). Only in the possibility of death was man made lower than angels, and then only for a short period of time.

c) The design for the future

In God's plan redeemed man will be gathered to Him and will no longer be lower than the angels.

(1) The possession of the kingdom

(a) Daniel 7:18—"The saints of the Most High shall take the kingdom, and possess the kingdom forever, even forever and ever." Who will take the kingdom? The saints of the Most High— redeemed men.

(b) Daniel 7:27—"The kingdom and dominion, and the greatness of the kingdom under the whole heaven, shall be given to the people of the saints of the Most High, whose kingdom is an everlasting kingdom, and all dominions shall serve and obey him." Isn't it fantastic that God has promised the ultimate kingdom to redeemed men? No wonder David said, "What is man, that thou art mindful of him?" (Ps. 8:4).

(2) The preview of the kingdom

(a) The equality between men and angels

In Luke 20 the Sadducees come to Jesus and ask Him questions about a hypothetical situation. A woman was married to a succession of brothers who kept replacing the previous one after he died. So they asked Jesus, "Whose wife will she be in heaven?" Jesus said, "The sons of this age marry, and are given in marriage; but they who shall be accounted worthy to obtain that age [the kingdom], and the resurrection from the dead, neither marry, nor are given in marriage. Neither can they die any more; for they are equal unto the angels" (vv. 34-36).

The hierarchy in the kingdom age will be completely different from what it is now. Man and angels will be equal. Man will be crowned king in Christ. And the earth will be redeemed. That's God's promise for the future.

(b) The reign of men over angels

Revelation 3:21 says that redeemed man will sit with Christ on His throne and rule. Ephesians 1:21 says that Christ will reign over principalities and powers. What are they? Angels. Since Christ reigns over angels in the kingdom, and we will sit on His throne with Him, we will reign over angels.

3. Given the right to rule

Hebrews 2:7 says, "Thou crownedst him with glory and honor." When God made Adam, who was pure and innocent, He gave him honor and glory. He was crowned with the *stephanōs*, which is the Greek word for the crown of rank. God crowned man king of the earth. Verse 8 says, "Thou hast put all things in subjection under his feet." In the first century, kings were always elevated above the people, and it was often said that the people were under the king's feet. When anyone approached the king, they would have to bow before him, sometimes even kissing his feet. Man has been given the right to rule as a king, and everything God has made has been put under his feet. Verses 7-8 say, "[Thou] didst set him over the works of thy hands; thou hast put all things in subjection under his feet." There is nothing that wasn't subject to man in the original creation.

God's revealed destiny for man was that he was made lower than angels for a short time. In innocence he was king over the undefiled earth. The earth served man—it fed him and provided everything he needed. But then something drastic happened.

II. MAN'S DESTINY RESTRICTED BY SIN (v. 8b)

"But now we see not yet all things put under him."

113

A. The Tragedy of Man

Unfortunately, a tragedy took place—Adam sinned.

1. The curses revealed

   *a)* To the serpent

   Genesis 3:14-15 says, "The Lord God said unto the serpent . . . thou art cursed above all cattle, and above every beast of the field; upon thy belly shalt thou go, and dust shalt thou eat all the days of thy life. And I will put enmity between thee and the woman, and between thy seed and her seed; he shall bruise thy head, and thou shalt bruise his heel." That is a prophecy concerning Christ's conflict with Satan.

   *b)* To the woman

   Genesis 3:16 says, "Unto the woman he said, I will greatly multiply thy sorrow and thy conception; in sorrow thou shalt bring forth children; and thy desire shall be to thy husband, and he shall rule over thee."

   *c)* To the man

   Genesis 3:17-19 says, "And unto Adam he said, Because thou hast hearkened unto the voice of thy wife, and hast eaten of the tree, of which I commanded thee, saying, Thou shalt not eat of it: cursed is the ground for thy sake; in sorrow shalt thou eat of it all the days of thy life; thorns also and thistles shall it bring forth to thee; and thou shalt eat the herb of the field; in the sweat of thy face shalt thou eat bread, till thou return unto the ground; for out of it wast thou taken: for dust thou art, and unto dust shalt thou return." Verses 22-24 say, "The Lord God said, Behold, the man is become as one of us, to know good and evil; and now, lest he put forth his hand, and take also of the tree of life, and eat, and live forever; therefore the Lord God sent him forth from the garden of Eden, to till the ground from where he was taken. So he drove out the man."

2. The crown removed

   *a)* The earth rules man

   What happened when Adam sinned? He immediately lost his crown. Man had been designed by God to have dominion over the earth. The earth supplied man's every need. He had only to accept and enjoy the earth as it provided for him. But then man sinned, and Satan usurped the crown. There was then a change in the chain of command. Man fell clear to the bottom, and now the earth rules man. We don't rule this world; it rules us.

Immediately after Adam sinned, there was murder among his own family. Polygamy soon followed. In the next few chapters of Genesis there is death. By the time we come to chapter 6, God destroys the world with a flood because it has become so debauched. The earth is now in the midst of conflict between holy and unholy angels. When man lost his crown, he was no longer a master of himself. He was totally sinful and became a slave to sin. The animals became subservient to man in the sense of fear and no longer in the sense of affection and service. Much of the animal kingdom is unable to be tamed. And instead of the ground yielding good things that are easy to eat, it now produces thorns, weeds, and other harmful things. Extremes of heat and cold, poisonous plants and reptiles, earthquakes, typhoons, floods, hurricanes, and disease were released upon men at the Fall. Man was no longer a king but a slave fighting all his life to exist. And he has been fighting a losing battle ever since. He is a dying creature and his earth is dying with him.

b) Satan rules the earth

Who is now the king of the earth? None other than the usurper who stole the crown, Satan himself. First John 5:19 says that the whole world lies in the wicked one. Man's destiny has been restricted by sin. The earth is ruled by Satan and his evil angels, who are in conflict with holy angels acting as God's ministers.

B. The Tragedy of the Earth

The earth is cursed, and it knows it. Romans 8 shows us the pain the earth is going through as it groans for its redemption. In Romans 8:18-19 Paul says, "I reckon that the sufferings of this present time are not worthy to be compared with the glory which shall be revealed in us. For the earnest expectation of the creation waiteth for the manifestation of the sons of God." The earth groans while waiting for the day when the redeemed will rule in God's glorious kingdom. Once the kingdom starts, the earth will be liberated from the

115

curse. Verse 20 says, "The creation was made subject to vanity, not willingly but by reason of him who hath subjected the same in hope." God subjected the earth to this vain curse that man might have trouble all his days. Man needed to know that God was aware of his sin and that he had to pay for his sin in part by fighting against the earth, which was originally designed to be subject to him. Verses 21-22 say, "The creation itself also shall be delivered from the bondage of corruption into the glorious liberty of the children of God. For we know that the whole creation groaneth and travaileth in pain together until now."

## Groaning with the Earth

The earth is aware of the curse that came upon it as a result of Adam's fall. It groans for the day that the sons of God will be manifest in the kingdom because it knows it will be liberated from the bondage of corruption. Man is subject to the earth. He sows but he doesn't know who will reap. He builds his cities and palaces but lightning or earthquake or flood or corruption destroys them. Man lives in jeopardy every hour. Just at the height of professional achievement, his brain may develop a tumor. Just at the brink of athletic triumph, he may be injured and become a helpless paralytic. Man fights against himself and against his earth. Every day we read about the distress of nations—about the impossibility of agreement between statesmen in a world that languishes in political and social conflict. The creation groans with the whine of pain from dumb animals, with the struggle of trees to combat disease and insects, and from the presence of hospitals that house the sick and dying victims of our cursed earth. But God never designed things to be that way.

No wonder the creation groans. Some day in the world to come hospitals will be closed, doctors will be out of business, and the ravenous nature of wild animals will be changed. Vegetation will no longer be stricken. The game of politics will be over. Wars will cease. The Bible says that men will "beat their swords into plowshares, and their spears into pruning hooks; nation shall not lift up sword against nation, neither shall they learn war any more" (Isa. 2:4). There is coming a day when in the wonderful plan of God, man will receive once again the dominion that he lost. He will be, as Jesus says in Luke 20:36, equal to angels in a permanent sense, and will reign over them forever.

## III. MAN'S DESTINY RECOVERED BY CHRIST (v. 9)

"But we see Jesus, who was made a little lower than the angels for the suffering of death, crowned with glory and honor, that he, by the grace of God, should taste death for every man."

Man's revealed destiny, restricted by sin, has been recovered by Christ. The ultimate curse of man's lost destiny is death. God said to Adam regarding the tree of the knowledge of good and evil, "In the day that thou eatest thereof thou shalt surely die" (Gen. 2:17).

A.  The Requirement of Death

In the restored kingdom we will be elevated again over a redeemed earth. But how is that going to happen? If we're all sinners, how are we ever going to be king again? The only payment for sin is death. Romans 6:23 says, "The wages of sin is death." The only way man can ever be a king again is to have the curse removed. The only way you can remove the curse is to pay the penalty of death. So if man is to be restored to his reign as king, he must die. Then he must be resurrected as a new man with sovereignty. But how? I can die, but I can't raise myself on my own.

B.  The Removal of the Curse

1.  The penalty is paid

Romans 6:10 says, "In that he [Christ] died, he died unto sin once; but in that he liveth, he liveth unto God." Jesus Christ is the one who died. Verse 3 says, "Know ye not that, as many of us as were baptized into Jesus Christ were baptized into his death?" Did you know that I died years ago? I died in the sense that Paul said he died in Galatians 2:20: "I am crucified with Christ." The moment I put my faith in Jesus Christ, I was identified with Him: I died on the cross, I was resurrected, and began to walk in newness of life. In my case, the curse was removed. I am a king! (Now I haven't inherited my dominion yet, but I'm patient!) The same is true for every one of you who know and love Jesus Christ. The kingdom belongs to the saints of the Most High, and He will get around to giving it to us in His time.

My present body will die someday, but I won't die. When my body dies, I'll be liberated into the presence of Jesus. Then again, maybe I'll be around when the rapture comes and He'll take me with Him, body and soul, into the kingdom.

117

2. Death is conquered

Jesus had to be a man to regain man's dominion. He was "made a little lower than the angels for the suffering of death" (Heb. 2:9). Why? Because He had to "taste death for every man" (v. 9). If a man had to die for his own sin, he would doom himself to hell and the crown could never be restored. So Jesus came and died and conquered death. As you and I identify ourselves with Jesus Christ in His death and receive Him as Savior, the curse is removed. We are made kings once again and restored to dominion.

C. The Results of Redemption

1. Angels minister to believers

Hebrews 1:14 says, "Are they not all ministering spirits [angels], sent forth to minister for them who shall be heirs of salvation?" According to that, I'm no longer in subjection to angels. As a king, angels minister to me. If you're a Christian, they minister to you. You're at least equal with them now, and in the kingdom you will be sovereign as you sit on Christ's throne and reign with Him.

2. Believers will reign on earth

Revelation 5:9-10 says, "They sang a new song, saying, Thou art worthy to take the scroll, and to open its seals; for thou wast slain, and hast redeemed us to God by thy blood out of every kindred, and tongue, and people, and nation; and hast made us unto our God a kingdom of priests, and we shall reign on the earth."

*a)* The kingdom revealed

If we're going to reign on earth as kings, there has to be a kingdom, and there will be one. It's described in Revelation 20:1-4: "I saw an angel come down from heaven, having the key of the bottomless pit and a great chain in his hand. And he laid hold on the dragon, that old serpent, who is the Devil and Satan, and bound him a thousand years, and cast him into the bottomless pit, and shut him up, and set a seal upon him, that he should deceive the nations no more, till the thousand years should be fulfilled. . . . And I saw thrones, and they sat upon them, and judgment was given unto them; and I saw the souls of them that were beheaded for the witness of Jesus, and for the word of God, and who had not worshiped the beast, neither his image, neither had received his mark upon their foreheads, or in their hands; and they lived and reigned with Christ a thousand years." We will be the ones on those thrones. And the One who made it all possible is the King of kings. What does the phrase "King of kings" mean? It means that we're the kings and that He's the King over us.

b) The earth redeemed

The earth will also be redeemed—the curse will be removed.

(1) Man

Isaiah 2:2-4 says, "It shall come to pass in the last days, that the mountain of the Lord's house shall be established in the top of the mountains, and shall be exalted above the hills; and all nations shall flow unto it. And many people shall go and say, Come ye, and let us go up to the mountain of the Lord, to the house of the God of Jacob; and he will teach us of his ways, and we will walk in his paths; for out of Zion shall go forth the law, and the word of the Lord from Jerusalem. And he shall judge among the nations, and shall rebuke many peoples; and they shall beat their swords into plowshares, and their spears into pruning hooks; nations shall not lift up sword against nation, neither shall they learn war any more." Men will be changed in the kingdom.

(2) Animals

Isaiah 11:6 says, "The wolf also shall dwell with the lamb, and the leopard shall lie down with the kid; and the calf and the young lion and the fatling together, and a little child shall lead them." Verses 8-9 continue, "And the nursing child shall play on the hole of the asp, and the weaned child shall put his hand on the adder's den. They shall not hurt nor destroy in all my holy mountain; for the earth shall be full of the knowledge of the Lord, as the waters cover the sea."

(3) Plants

Isaiah 35:1-2 says, "The wilderness and the solitary place shall be glad for them; and the desert shall rejoice, and blossom like the rose. It shall blossom abundantly."

There is going to be a different world. And man is going to be restored to the place of a king.

Notice that Hebrews 2:9 says, "By the grace of God." God's grace—God's love for us—is the key. Christ tasted death for you and me. He did it to recover your lost destiny. If you've been groping around trying to figure out why you exist, I hope you know why you do now. There's no reason for you to be a slave or a pauper, because you can be a king! Men today ask, "What is man?" The idolator and the animist say, "Man is inferior to birds and animals, to creeping things, and to stones and sticks." They bow down and worship such things. The materialist says, "Man is a chance product." But God says, "Man is the king of the earth." It is only for a little time that he has been made lower than the angels. Some day he will be equal to them and sit on the throne of Jesus Christ, reigning with Him in His kingdom. I trust you'll be there reigning with Christ.

## Focusing on the Facts

1. How were people saved in the Old Testament (see p. 105)?
2. What is a type? What are some of the Old Testament types that were fulfilled in Christ (see pp. 105-6)?
3. Name three things that Hebrews 2:5–9 accomplishes (see p. 107).
4. Who is going to rule in the future world? Who has the rule in our present world (see pp. 108-9)?
5. Why is the present earth under the rule of angels (see p. 109)?
6. What was probably the writer's intention when he said, "But one in a certain place testified" (Heb. 2:6; see pp. 109–10)?
7. What is God's revealed destiny for man (see p. 110)?
8. In what way was man made lower than angels (see p. 111)?
9. What does the phrase "a little lower" in Hebrews 2:7 mean? What significance does that have for man in God's chain of command (see p. 111)?
10. What will the hierarchy be in the kingdom age (see p. 113)?
11. What were the various curses that God pronounced as a result of man's sin (Gen. 3:14-19; see p. 114)?
12. What happened to God's chain of command when Adam sinned (see pp. 114-15)?

13. Describe the pain that the earth is undergoing in its unredeemed state (Rom. 8:18-22; see pp. 115-16).
14. What does man have to do if he wants to be restored to his reign as king? Explain how that is accomplished (see p. 117).
15. Describe the changes that will take place when the curse is removed from the earth (see pp. 119-20).

## Pondering the Principles

1. Match the following types with their corresponding verses:

| | |
|---|---|
| a. The red heifer | 1. Exodus 40:21 (Heb. 10:20) |
| b. The brazen altar | 2. Genesis 2:9 (Rev. 22:2) |
| c. The Mercy Seat | 3. Numbers 19:2-6 (Heb. 9:13-14) |
| d. The veil | 4. Exodus 27:1-2 (Heb. 13:10) |
| e. Cities of refuge | 5. Exodus 25:17-22 (Heb. 4:15-16) |
| f. The tree of life | 6. Numbers 35:6 (Heb. 6:18) |

What do each of those types prefigure? What new insight have you gained from this small study of types?

2. How has your perspective of your future changed as a result of this chapter? Thank God for that future, and thank Christ for securing it for you. Now that you know what your destiny is and how it was lost and then restored, how would you approach an unbeliever who is searching for meaning to his life? Utilize the main points in this lesson to frame your own presentation for leading someone toward recovering his lost destiny.

# 7
## Our Perfect Savior

### Outline

Introduction
A. The Problems
   1. How could Jesus be superior to angels?
   2. How could Jesus be a victim of death?
B. The Purpose

Lesson
I. Our Substitute (v. 9)
  A. God's Choice
  B. Christ's Choice
    1. The concept of His humiliation
    2. The extent of His humiliation
    3. The purpose of His humiliation
      *a*) The accomplishment
        (1) Galatians 4:4-5
        (2) 2 Corinthians 5:15
      *b*) The analogy
    4. The motive of His humiliation
      *a*) The provision of grace
      *b*) The prompting of grace
        (1) John 10:18
        (2) 1 John 4:10
    5. The result of His humiliation
      *a*) Hebrews 5:4-5
      *b*) Philippians 2:9-10
      *c*) Ephesians 1:21
II. Our Captain of Salvation (v. 10)
  A. Agreeing with God's Character
  B. Blazing the Trail to God
    1. The perfect pattern
      *a*) His obedience
      *b*) His suffering for others

c)   His death and resurrection
       2.   The perfect leader
III.  Our Sanctifier (vv. 11-13)
     A.  The Position of Brotherhood (v. 11)
         1.   Made holy in Christ
         2.   Made one in Christ
         3.   Made brothers in Christ
              a)   The price
              b)   The promotion
     B.  The Proof of Brotherhood (vv. 12-13)
         1.   Christ's declaration (v. 12)
         2.   Christ's dependence (v. 13)
IV.  Our Conqueror over Satan (vv. 14-15)
     A.  Christ Removed Satan's Weapon of Death (v. 14)
         1.   The dominion of death
         2.   The destruction of death
     B.  Christ Released the Saints from the Fear of Death (v. 15)
V.   Our Sympathizer (vv. 16-18)
     A.  His Nationality (v. 16)
     B.  His Mission (vv. 17-18)
         1.   Reconciliation
         2.   Sympathy
              a)   Our dependence on Christ
              b)   His degree of temptation

## Introduction

A newspaper article once hailed the arrival of the "Son of God": Guru Maharaj Ji, the young leader of the Divine Light Mission. But that is nothing new because he takes his place in a long line of would-be saviors of the world. They go back to men like Theudas, who tried to split the waters of the Jordan River and couldn't (Josephus, *Antiquities* 20.5.1). There are even modern-day "saviors" like Hitler. Someday another individual will claim to be the world's savior, and he is known in Scripture as the Antichrist. But unfortunately for all would-be saviors—and fortunately for us—there is only one perfect Savior: Jesus Christ. The apostle Peter said, "Neither is there salvation in any other; for there is no other name under heaven given among men, whereby we must be saved" (Acts 4:12). But how can we know that Jesus Christ is, in fact, the perfect Savior? What qualifies Him? The complete answer to the validity of His claim is in Hebrews 2:9-18.

The Holy Spirit wrote Hebrews through an unknown author primarily to the Jewish people, but that does not mean it isn't for

124

anyone else. To prove that Jesus Christ is the Son of God, the mediator of a new and better covenant, the Holy Spirit must prove to the Jew that Christ is better than all the issues that accompany the Old Covenant. We've learned that the Old Covenant was mediated to men by angels. Therefore, the Holy Spirit must prove to the Jewish mind that Christ is superior to angels, which He did in the first two chapters of Hebrews.

A. The Problems

There were questions still lingering after the Holy Spirit's presentation in Hebrews 1:1—2:9.

1. How could Jesus be superior to angels?

The Holy Spirit had been attempting to prove that Jesus is better than angels. But the problem that stayed with the Jew is: How could Jesus be better than angels since He was a man who died? Angels never die, and they are certainly higher than men. The theological problem that the Jews faced was relating the humanity of Christ and His death to His superiority over angels, who cannot die (Luke 20:36).

Hebrews 2:9 says, "But we see Jesus, who was made a little lower." We determined from the Greek text that the phrase "a little lower" was a connotation for time. Verse 9 is saying that Jesus became less for a brief period of time. By nature Christ is greater than angels. It was only for a little time in His incarnation that He became less to accomplish a specific purpose.

2. How could Jesus be a victim of death?

How could Jesus die if He was the Messiah—the Anointed of God? Whenever the Word of God was preached to the Jews, as in Acts 17:2-3, it was necessary for them to know why Christ had to suffer. Paul told the Corinthians that the cross was a stumbling block to the Jews (1 Cor. 1:23).

B. The Purpose

In Hebrews 2:9-18 the Holy Spirit defends the incarnation. He tells us why Jesus became lower than angels for a little time: He came to die. Those soft baby hands fashioned by the Holy Spirit in Mary's womb were made to have two great nails put through them. Those pink and white chubby feet were to walk up a hill and be nailed to a cross. That sacred head was made to wear a crown. His tender body wrapped in swaddling clothes would be ripped open by a spear to reveal a broken heart. The death of Christ was no accident—He was born to die.

Jesus did not lose His identity by becoming lower than angels. When God created man in his innocence, He gave him dominion over the earth. But man sinned and he immediately lost his dominion. Jesus Christ came to die to remove the curse so man could regain his dominion. So there was a definite purpose in Jesus' coming to die—He came to restore the crown. But to do that He had to come as a man. Even though He was lower than angels, He accomplished something no angel could—the restoration of man.

There are five perfections that Christ's humanness and death brought about. Jesus became our substitute, our captain of salvation, our sanctifier, our conqueror over Satan, and our sympathizer. He is our perfect Savior. The death of Christ is not hard to explain at all—it was the purpose for His incarnation.

## Lesson

### I. OUR SUBSTITUTE (v. 9)

"But we see Jesus, who was made a little lower than the angels for the suffering of death, crowned with glory and honor, that he, by the grace of God, should taste death for every man."

Christ died in our place. The first and foremost reason for the incarnation is that He might taste death on behalf of every man. He came to die in my place—to be my substitute.

#### A. God's Choice

The prophet Ezekiel said, "The soul that sinneth, it shall die" (Ezek. 18:4). The Bible lays down that same principle in the New Testament: "The wages of sin is death" (Rom. 6:23). Sin brings death. God had two options: Either let man die and pay for his own sin, or allow a substitute to take man's punishment and die in his place. The latter was His design. He sent the second person of the Trinity (God humbled Himself) to earth to die a substitutionary death for me. That doctrine is important to affirm, because modern liberal theology does not adhere to it. It claims that Jesus died as an

126

example, like a martyr dying for some cause. But He died as a substitute for your death and mine.

B. Christ's Choice

1. The concept of His humiliation

For Jesus Christ to die for man, He had to become what man is. That's the purpose of the incarnation. God became man to be a substitute for man's death. Thus He freed man to live a life with God. That's how simple the gospel is. It is a stunning concept to realize that the creator of angels, the Lord of hosts, should become lower than angels for our sakes. Now that's humility! Verse 9 says that after becoming our substitute, He was lifted up to glory and honor.

2. The extent of His humiliation

Hebrews 2:9 says that Jesus became "a little lower than the angels for the suffering of death." Jesus came to do precisely what no angel could ever do, and that is to die. The phrase "for the suffering of death" indicates that His exit from the land of the living was not calm and peaceful; it was accompanied by outward torture and inward agony.

3. The purpose of His humiliation

   a) The accomplishment

   Here is the purpose of Christ's death: That He "should taste death for every man" (v. 9). He drank its bitter cup. The death He tasted was the curse of sin. Jesus suffered the total agony of every soul in hell for all eternity in a few hours on the cross. That was the depth of His suffering. He was guilty of nothing, but He suffered for everything because He chose to be our substitute.

   (1) Galatians 4:4-5—"When the fullness of the time was come, God sent forth his Son, made of a woman, made under the law, to redeem them that were under the law." God sent His Son to redeem men.

   (2) 2 Corinthians 5:15—"He died for all, that they who live should not henceforth live unto themselves, but unto him who died for them, and rose again." Jesus Christ purposed to die as a substi-

127

tute for every man. It is only as a result of the Son's tasting death that we are free from death.

b) The analogy

Historically, kings have had someone taste their food and drink their wine before they consumed it. The cup of poison that belonged to us was drained to the dregs by Jesus Christ before it could ever touch our lips. He substituted His death for ours, releasing us from sin to live with God.

4. The motive of His humiliation

a) The provision of grace

Hebrews 2:9 tells us that God's grace moved Jesus Christ to suffer for us. Do you know what grace is? It is free lovingkindness. What we did not deserve—salvation—we received, and what we did deserve—death—we did not receive.

b) The prompting of grace

God's great, unbounded love prompted a gracious deed on our behalf. Solely on the basis of His own good pleasure and His sovereign will Jesus died (Eph. 1:5). He did not die by the hands of men or by the deed of Satan alone but by the determinate counsel and foreknowledge of God (Acts 2:23).

(1) John 10:18—Jesus said, "No man taketh [life] from me, but I lay it down of myself."

(2) 1 John 4:10—"Herein is love, not that we loved God, but that he loved us, and sent his Son to be the propitiation [satisfaction] for our sins."

5. The result of His humiliation

Jesus was "crowned with glory and honor" (Heb. 2:9). After Jesus accomplished His substitutionary death, He was exalted to the right hand of the Father and now sits on a throne to reign forever.

a) Hebrews 5:4-5—"No man taketh this honor unto himself, but he that is called of God, as was Aaron. So also Christ glorified not himself to be made an high priest, but he that said unto him, Thou art my Son, today have I begotten thee." Christ didn't glorify Himself; God glorified Him.

*b)* Philippians 2:9-10—"God also hath highly exalted him, and given him a name which is above every name, that at the name of Jesus every knee should bow."

*c)* Ephesians 1:21—Jesus Christ has been set over "all principality, and power, and might, and dominion, and every name that is named."

The result of Christ's humiliation was His exaltation.

The writer of Hebrews is explaining to his Jewish readers that believers don't apologize for the cross because it magnifies the Lord. That He was a man who died is no problem because He condescended to do so. Christ's humiliation and death is far from being something we are ashamed of; it is something we glory in. Jesus became a perfect substitute by becoming a man. If He had not died for us, we would die in our sins (John 8:24).

## II. OUR CAPTAIN OF SALVATION (v. 10)

"For it became him [it agreed with His nature], for whom are all things, and by whom are all things, in bringing many sons unto glory, to make the captain of their salvation perfect through sufferings."

God not only made all things, but He made it all for Himself because He deserves the glory. And God brought many sons to glory because His design is to bring men to Himself. Jesus had to become a man and He had to suffer and die to be the perfect provider of salvation.

A. Agreeing with God's Character

The phrase "it became him" means that what God did through Christ was consistent with His character.

1. Wisdom

God is wisdom. And the cross was a masterpiece of wisdom. God solved a problem that no finite brain or angels could hope to solve: reconciling sinful man to a holy God.

2. Holiness

God showed His hatred for sin on the cross.

3. Power

The cross was the greatest display of power that God ever gave. Christ endured in a few hours what it would take an eternity to expend on sinners.

4. Love

5. Grace

Christ's death on the cross agreed with God's grace because it was substitutionary.

6. Nature

God's work of salvation was totally consistent with His nature.

God's desire was to bring many sons to His glory. To do that, He had to tell us how to get there. But more than that, He had to have someone to take us. It wouldn't have done us a bit of good if Jesus had arrived here and left a map to heaven.

B. Blazing the Trail to God

The Greek word for "captain" in Hebrews 2:10 is *archēgos*, which means "pioneer" or "leader." In Acts 3:15 and Acts 5:31 it's translated "prince." It is translated "captain" in many verses. It often refers to someone who does something that someone else enters into or benefits from. For example, it's used of a man who founds a family that others are born into. It's used of a man who founds a city in which others come to live. It was commonly used of a pioneer who blazed a trail for others to follow. The *archēgos* never stood at the rear giving orders; he was always out front blazing the trail. Christ has gone before us. He is our trailblazer.

1. The perfect pattern

   a) His obedience

   Hebrews 5:8-9 says, "Though he were a Son, yet learned he obedience by the things which he suffered; and being made perfect, he became the author of eternal salvation unto all them that obey him." By His obedience Jesus blazed the trail of obedience for us to follow.

   b) His suffering for others

   The apostle Peter said, "Hereunto were ye called, because Christ also suffered for us" (1 Pet. 2:21).

   c) His death and resurrection

   Jesus said, "Because I live, ye shall live also" (John 14:19). He also said, "Whosoever liveth and believeth in me shall never die" (John 11:26).

Jesus is the *Archēgos* of salvation. He blazed the trail to God. He didn't stay in the rear and tell us how to get there; He went out in front. All we have to do is take His hand and let Him lead us into the presence of God.

2. The perfect leader

God made Christ lower than angels for a brief time so He could come down to us, take our hand, and be the perfect leader. Only the perfect pioneer could take us into the presence of the Father. It is only when you put your hand in the nail-scarred hand of Jesus Christ that you'll ever enter into the presence of God. You'll never find your way on your own. Men have tried and failed.

Through death Jesus became the perfect leader. The trail got rough at the point of death. That's where we couldn't make it. But Jesus says, "Because I live, ye shall live also" (John 14:19). G. B. Hardy in his book *Countdown: A Time to Choose* says that the following are the ultimate questions in the world: Has anyone ever cheated death? And if he did, did he leave the way open for me ([Chicago: Moody, 1971], p. 32)? Yes, someone did cheat death; His name is Jesus Christ. And He did leave the way open for us. All you have to do is put your hand in His and He'll lead you out of death. You'll say with the apostle Paul, "O death, where is thy sting? O grave, where is thy victory?" (1 Cor. 15:55). There isn't any. Christ has given us the victory. He had to be a man to come into our world and lead us out. He had to conquer the barrier between us and God, which was sin. And He conquered it by bearing the punishment of death, thus leaving the way open to eternal life with God.

## III. OUR SANCTIFIER (vv. 11-13)

A. The Position of Brotherhood (v.11)

"For both he that sanctifieth [Christ] and they who are sanctified are all of one, for which cause he is not ashamed to call them brethren."

1. Made holy in Christ

Verse 11 means that Christians are holy. You may think you're not holy, but you are. I'm not talking about your practice; I'm talking about your position: Before God you are holy. You may not always act holy, but you are in His sight. Just as a child may not always act like the son of his father, he is nonetheless still his son. The righteousness of Christ has been placed before God on your behalf, and that makes you holy. There are two truths in the New

131

Testament: positional truth and practical truth—what you are and how you act. Positionally, you are holy and perfect. Colossians 2:10 says, "Ye are complete in him." Yet practically we've all got a long way to go.

2.  Made one in Christ

    Hebrews 2:11 says, "He that sanctifieth and they who are sanctified are all of one." Did you know that we're all one with Christ? The apostle Paul calls us joint heirs with Christ (Rom. 8:17). We are one with Christ because His righteousness is our righteousness.

3.  Made brothers in Christ

    As a result of being one with Christ, He's not ashamed to call us brothers. What an overwhelming truth! The Son of God calls me brother and is not ashamed to do so.

    a)  The price

        By conquering sin through His death, Christ placed His righteousness on us in an eternal, positional sense. Thus, we became holy. He could never have done that had He not paid the penalty for sin. He had to die to be our sanctifier. The Greek word for "sanctified" is *hagiazō*, which means "to make holy." Only Jesus Christ can make a person holy.

        Hebrews 10:10 says, "By which will we are sanctified [made holy] through the offering of the body of Jesus Christ once for all." We were made holy through His sacrifice. Verse 14 says, "For by one offering he hath perfected forever them that are sanctified." Positionally, you are as pure as God is pure, righteous as Christ is righteous, and therefore entitled to be called a brother of Jesus Christ. That is a good indication of what God's grace is like. Out of love He stooped to pick us up and give us righteous equality with Jesus Christ. The Bible says, "[God] hath made [Christ], who knew no sin, to be sin for us, that we might be made the righteousness of God in him" (2 Cor. 5:21).

    b)  The promotion

        Hebrews 11:16 says, "But now they desire a better country, that is, an heavenly; wherefore, God is not ashamed to be called their God." Can you imagine God being happy to be called your God? Do you know why? It is not because of who you are, but because of who you are in Christ. Your righteousness is His.

In Romans 1:16 the apostle Paul says, "I am not ashamed of the gospel of Christ." But isn't it sad that although God is never ashamed to call us His own, we are often ashamed to call Him ours? Who has the right to be ashamed of whom? When I realize that Jesus is not ashamed to call me His brother, and that God is not ashamed to say He is my God, that thrills my heart. It makes me well aware that I stand in the righteousness of Jesus Christ and not my own, which is at best filthy rags (Isa. 64:6). Let me add that all men are not Christ's brothers. Only those who by faith in Jesus Christ have His righteousness are related to Him.

B.  The Proof of Brotherhood (vv. 12-13)

The Holy Spirit proves the brotherhood aspect by using Old Testament quotations, as He does throughout Hebrews. He quotes the words of Christ spoken to the Father in the Old Testament.

1.  Christ's declaration (v.12)

"I will declare thy name unto my brethren, in the midst of the church [congregation] will I sing praise unto thee."

This quote from Psalm 22:22 is a picture of Jesus Christ calling believers His brothers in the Old Testament. Psalm 22 deals with the crucifixion and the resurrection. Jesus is pictured in post-resurrection joy with His brothers. And that tells the Jewish reader that the idea of the Messiah as a brother is right out of the Old Testament. That is a convincing argument for the Jewish individual. So often in Scripture, especially in the book of Hebrews, the writer turns to the Old Testament to corroborate truth.

2.  Christ's dependence (v. 13)

"And again, I will put my trust in him. And again, Behold I and the children whom God hath given me."

Hebrews 2:13 is a quote from Isaiah 8:17-18. Christ admitted that He lived by faith, just like His brothers. Jesus Christ is our brother not in nature or power, for we are human and He is divine, but in righteousness and faith. When Jesus was in this world, He learned the obedience of faith and thus became a perfect Savior. It's a tremendous thing to realize that when we are called to walk by faith, submit ourselves, and live in dependence on God, we can follow the path Jesus walked. He said, "The Son can do nothing of himself, but what he seeth the Father do; for whatever things he doeth, these also doeth the Son in the same manner" (John 5:19).

Brotherhood with Jesus means we have His righteousness and walk as He did: by faith.

## IV. OUR CONQUEROR OVER SATAN (vv. 14-15)

Someone had to break Satan's power over us. If we were to be free to live with God and experience what He has, someone had to shatter the power that held us. And what is Satan's power over men? Death. Sin is a part of it, but death is the ultimate weapon. If Satan can hang on to a man until he dies, he has him forever. So someone had to conquer death to conquer Satan.

### A. Christ Removed Satan's Weapon of Death (v. 14)

"Forasmuch, then, as the children are partakers of flesh and blood, he also himself likewise took part of the same, that through death he might destroy him that had the power of death, that is, the devil."

1. The dominion of death

   Satan's hold on men is physical, spiritual, and eternal death. Satan knows God requires death for sin. Satan knows that all died in Adam—that death entered as a principle of life. He wants to hold onto men until they die because once they're dead, they cannot escape.

2. The destruction of death

   God needed to wrest the power of death from Satan's hand. Jesus came to accomplish that purpose. But how was He to do that? Simple: conquer death. If you've got a greater weapon than Satan, then his weapon is useless. You can't fight a machine gun with a bow and arrow. If all Satan has is death, and God has something greater, then Satan's weapon is useless. Jesus provided something better than death: life. Jesus destroyed death. Notice that verse 14 says, "Through death he might destroy him." It was through death that Christ destroyed Satan's power of death. How could that happen? Because Jesus rose again proving He could conquer it. That's why He said, "Because I live, ye shall live also" (John 14:19).

Jesus left the pathway open. The resurrection of Jesus Christ provides the believer with eternal life. It's the only thing that could have done it. Satan had dominion over all men in the form of death, but Jesus shattered that dominion.

## The Significance of the Incarnation

Hebrews 2:14 says, "The children are *partakers* of flesh and blood" (emphasis added). The Greek word translated "partakers" is *koinōneō*, from which we get the words *fellowship* and *communion*. It refers to a partnership. We are made of flesh and blood. That's our nature. Verse 14 says, "[Christ] also himself likewise took part of the same." The Greek word translated "part" is not *koinōneo* but *metechō*, which means He took hold of something that was not His own nature. Christ is not flesh and blood by nature, but He willingly took hold of it that He might die in our place.

By rising from the dead, Jesus smashed Satan's power. Revelation 1:18 says that Jesus Christ has "the keys of hades and of death." Jesus became the death of death. S. W. Gandy said,

> He hell in hell laid low,
> Made sin, He sin o'erthrew,
> Bowed to the grave, destroyed it so,
> And death by dying slew.

Jesus Christ conquered death in His resurrection and left the way open for us. But He had to be a man to do it.

B. Christ Released the Saints from Fear of Death (v. 15)

"And deliver them who, through fear of death, were all their lifetime subject to bondage."

All through their lives men are subject to the bondage of the fear of death. It's a horrible fear—the king of terrors. But when you receive Jesus Christ, death holds no fear. We're released from the bondage of our fear. You can actually look forward to death in that sense. The apostle Paul said, "To live is Christ, and to die is gain" (Phil. 1:21). It's a promotion. He didn't mind staying, but he knew that to be with Christ is far better (vv. 22-23). We say with Paul, "O death, where is thy sting? O grave, where is thy victory?" (1 Cor. 15:55). Death holds no fear for believers. It simply releases us into the presence of Jesus Christ. We are no longer in fear of death

135

because Jesus has conquered it. We've placed our hand in the hand of the captain of our salvation, and He'll lead us out of the grave. But He never could have done it if he hadn't become lower than angels for a little while.

## V. OUR SYMPATHIZER (vv. 16-18)

### A. His Nationality (v. 16)

"For verily he took not on him the nature of angels, but he took on him the seed of Abraham."

What's the significance of that? He didn't come to redeem angels. If He was to redeem man, He had to become a man. So He took on Himself the form of Abraham's seed and became a Jew. There are songs that say Jesus is black, or Jesus is white, or that He's all colors. But Jesus was a Jew. Someone once wrote, "How odd of God to choose the Jews." (He concluded, "Not so, you know, His Son was one.") But if He'd chosen another race, people would ask, "Why did He choose them?" The Bible says that God chose them because He loved them (Deut. 7:7-8).

### B. His Mission (vv. 17-18)

"Wherefore, in all things it behooved him to be made like his brethren, that he might be a merciful and faithful high priest in things pertaining to God, to make reconciliation for the sins of the people. For in that he himself had suffered being tempted, he is able to help them that are tempted."

1. Reconciliation

   Jesus became a man because He came to reconcile men. The high priest's job was to represent men before God. Jesus came to take men into the presence of God.

2. Sympathy

   Jesus also came to help those who are tempted. He wanted to feel everything we've ever felt that He might be a merciful and faithful high priest. He came not only to save us but also to sympathize with us.

   a) Our dependence on Christ

      Timothy had many problems. Paul told him, "Stir up the gift of God, which is in thee" (2 Tim. 1:6). Timothy needed to fan the flame. He was also bothered by heretics and by those who were upset at him because he was young. Paul said, "Let no man

136

despise thy youth, but be thou an example [to] the believers" (1 Tim. 4:12). Timothy was feeling defeated, and he may have had an ulcer because Paul said, "Use a little wine for thy stomach's sake" (1 Tim. 5:23). Timothy did have many problems, but Paul's final advice was, "Remember . . . Jesus Christ, of the seed of David" (2 Tim. 2:8). One of the things Timothy needed to remember was Christ's humanity and know that whatever he was experiencing, Jesus had experienced before him.

When the going gets tough, you can get down on your knees and say, "Lord, You remember what You went through when You were here. I'm going through it now." Know that He knows what you're going through. And be encouraged by this: "There hath no temptation taken you but such as is common to man; but God is faithful, who will not permit you to be tempted above that ye are able, but will, with the temptation, also make the way to escape" (1 Cor. 10:13). Isn't it wonderful to be able to lean on someone who has been through a problem like yours, knowing that he has experienced victory? I'm sure you know how it feels to tell someone about your problem when they can't relate to it—you feel like you wasted your time telling them about it. But when you find someone who can understand, you feel like you've found a rock to lean on.

b) His degree of temptation

Jesus didn't just arrive in the world and die; He "was in all points tempted like as we are, yet without sin" (Heb. 4:15). He wanted to be a merciful, faithful, and sympathetic high priest. Jesus was hungry, thirsty, and overcome with fatigue. He slept. He was taught. He grew. He loved. He was astonished. He marveled. He was glad, angry, indignant, and sarcastic. He was grieved and troubled. He was overcome by future events. He exercised faith. He read Scripture. He prayed all night. He sighed in His heart when He saw another man in illness. Tears fell from His eyes when His heart ached. He felt everything you'll ever feel, but He felt it to a degree that one who never gives in to temptation feels. He felt temptation to its extreme on every occasion. Most of us never know what degree temptation can go to because we succumb about three-quarters of the way down the line at best. Jesus never sinned. He took the full shot of every temptation that ever came His way, and He felt every pain that you and I will ever feel and more. Why did He do that? So that we might have a merciful and faithful high priest who can "be touched with the feeling of our infirmities" (Heb. 4:15).

I don't want a cosmic God who is indifferent to me. I want someone who knows where I hurt and where I feel pain. So Jesus had to become lower than angels to be the kind of Savior you can go to for sympathy in addition to salvation. Jesus is our perfect Savior.

## Focusing on the Facts

1. What were two questions that might still have been on the mind of the Jew even after the discussion in Hebrews 1:1—2:9 (see p. 125)?
2. What are five perfections that Christ's humanness and death brought about (see p. 126)?
3. What were God's two options for dealing with man's sin? Which option did He choose (see p. 126)?
4. What kind of death did Christ endure (see p. 127)?
5. What was the purpose of Christ's death (see p. 127)?
6. What was the motive behind Christ's death on the cross (see p. 128)?
7. According to Hebrews 2:10, it agreed with God's character to make Christ the captain of our salvation through suffering. What aspects of God's character did it agree with (see pp. 129-30)?
8. Explain how Christ is the captain of our salvation (see pp. 130-31).
9. Who makes the Christian holy? Explain (Heb. 2:11; see p. 131).
10. How are Christians made holy (Heb. 10:10; see p. 132)?
11. Why is God not ashamed to be called our God, or Christ to call us brothers (see p. 132)?
12. Explain how the Holy Spirit proves the Christian's brotherhood with Christ in Hebrews 2:12-13 (see pp. 133-34)?
13. What is the ultimate weapon that Satan holds over man (see p. 134)?
14. How did Christ destroy Satan's weapon (Heb. 2:14; see p. 134)?
15. What is man's greatest fear? What is the only way a person can effectively deal with it (Heb. 2:15; see p. 135)?
16. Explain how Jesus can sympathize with our problems (Heb. 2:17-18; see pp. 136-37).

## Pondering the Principles

1. As the captain of our salvation, Christ not only blazed a trail to God but also set a pattern that we can follow. Look up the following verses: John 15:9-13; 1 Peter 1:21; 1 John 2:29. Determine what pattern of behavior Jesus established in each of those verses. How well are you following the pattern Jesus set? Memorize one verse each day for the next three days. As you do that, be thinking of ways you can follow that pattern, and then do it.

2. Read Romans 8:15-17 and Hebrews 2:11. All believers are children of God, brothers of Christ, and joint heirs with Christ. Those special relationships bring about mighty blessings in the life of a believer. To find out what those blessings are, read Ephesians 1 and record every blessing that comes with being in the family of God.

3. One of the things that can be most destructive to Christians is times of discouragement. That's when we really need someone to lean on, but sometimes a loving brother or sister in Christ is not available. Even if one is, Christ wants you to lean on Him first because He is the best one to deal with your pain. To help you through such times, memorize 1 Corinthians 10:13: "No temptation has overtaken you but such as is common to man; and God is faithful, who will not allow you to be tempted beyond what you are able, but with the temptation will provide the way of escape also, that you may be able to endure it" (NASB*).

*New American Standard Bible.

# Scripture Index

142

Moody Press, a ministry of the Moody Bible Institute, is designed for education, evangelization, and edification. If we may assist you in knowing more about Christ and the Christian life, please write us without obligation: Moody Press, c/o MLM, Chicago, Illinois 60610.